HELL ON EARTH

By

F. HAYDN HORNSEY

A Reprint of the 1930 Edition

With an Introduction by R. S. Richardson

INTRODUCTION TO THE REPRINTED EDITION

Frank Haydn Hornsey, the author of *Hell on Earth*, was born in Wellingborough, Northamptonshire, on the 23rd August 1898. He died in Earls Barton, Northamptonshire, on the 22nd April 1979.

The son of Frank Herbert and Annie Elizabeth Hornsey (née Northern), he had two brothers, Harold and Geoffrey Roland, and a sister, Doris Evelyn. He attended Victoria Council School in Wellingborough. On leaving school he was employed as a farm worker until being conscripted into the Army on 19th November 1917. Private F. H. Hornsey, (No.51289), joined the 3rd (Reserve) Battalion, Suffolk Regiment – a training unit – based at Felixstowe. After the training period he was drafted to a New Army battalion, the 11th (Service) Battalion, Suffolk Regiment (Cambridgeshire).

Private F. H. Hornsey was demobilised and transferred to the reserve on 12th February 1919.

Fig. 1 Frank Haydn Hornsey c.1930

Hell on Earth was published by Chapman and Hall in 1930. This book was an account based on his war experiences in France and Belgium. Between 1st January and 13th June 1918, he had kept a diary (Fig. 2). This Boots Pocket Diary – with brief entries written in pencil – covers the period of training in Felixstowe, 1st January – 4th April, followed by the period on active service in France and Belgium, 5th April – 13th June. This diary must have been referred to when he was writing *Hell on Earth*. The book was written when he lived at 24 Broadway, Wellingborough.

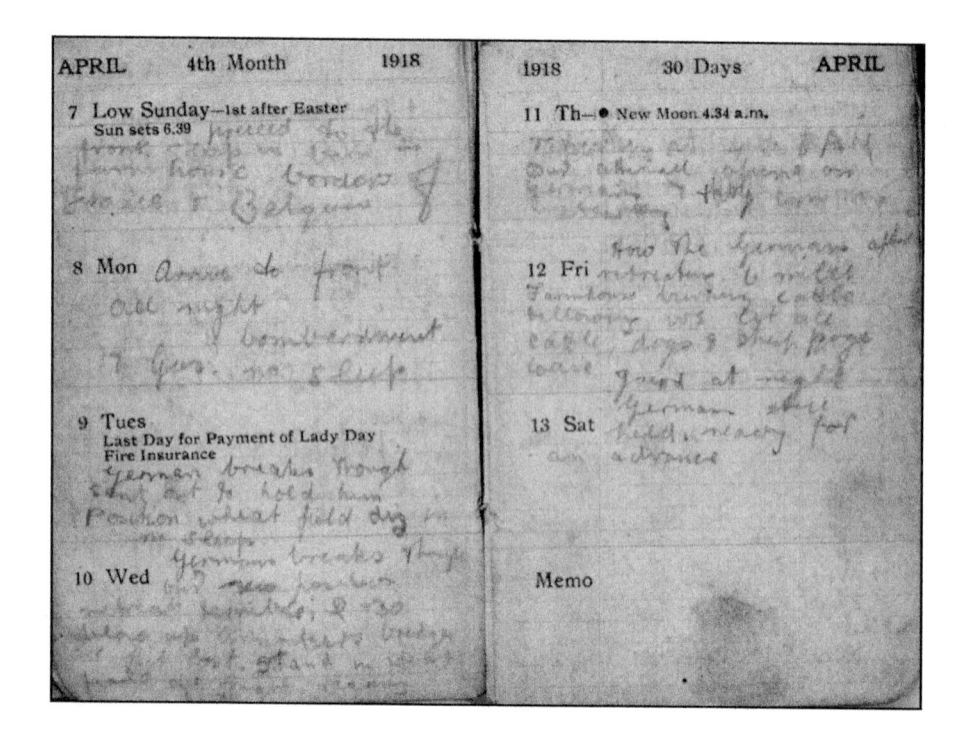

Fig. 2 F Haydn Hornsey's Pocket Diary 7th-13th April 1918

ii

The book was well received in the local press at the time:–

> Mr. F H. Hornsey, the Wellingborough author of the latest war book, *Hell on Earth*, has literally achieved fame overnight. His initial venture into literary realms promises to be a tremendous success. An unassuming young man – he is still in his early thirties – Mr. Hornsey joined up at the age of 18 in November 1917, and played a part with thousands of others in the dark days of Armageddon that followed. Within a few hours of landing in France in the spring of 1918, he was on the scene of desperate fighting on the Armentières front, with the Suffolk Regiment.
> After twelve years, as he told our reporter, he came to write his impressions of that *Hell on Earth*. The book was written within twelve months and is described by its author as "just an adventure"
> "Perhaps it may seem absurd," he said, "but ever since I finished with the Army I felt I would like to record my experiences, and after so many books have been published I have been tempted to come out in print. It is absolutely my first attempt and I have had no lessons or tuition of any sort."
> "The book is absolutely true from beginning to end, and I have not exaggerated anything. All the characters had their counterpart in real life, although, of course, the names have been changed. One at any rate is residing in Northamptonshire, and may easily recognise himself!"
> Mr. Hornsey is confident that his book will do a great deal of good on one particular point. He pays especial tribute to the officers and told our representative that he had never come into contact with drink and whisky-sodden officers as portrayed in other war works. *Hell on Earth* vindicates to a great extent these gallant officers whose reputations may have been somewhat besmirched…
> I asked Mr. Hornsey if he believed the publication of war books was of use in promoting peace. He replied that they were. "It is only right," he said, "that those of the younger generation who were too young at the time to understand the

horrors, should know what war means." (***Northamptonshire Advertiser*, May 1930.)**

NOTES OF THE WEEK Friday May 30th 1930 "Someone has put on record that there are three difficulties in authorship: to write anything worth the publishing, to find honest men to publish, and to get sensible men to read it. This week a young Wellingborough author has made his bow with a book Hell on Earth, the contents of which would seem to justify the title chosen. Just now, when there has been a super-abundance of books on the war, it might have been thought there was no room for another book of this kind, but the writer, Mr. F. Haydn Hornsey, felt that he had a story to tell, and set about telling it. He did not attempt to try and deal with the many issues which were involved in the Great War, but he was content to confine his writing to that which came under his own eye and in which he had a part. Judged from a literary standpoint, the book might be deemed lacking in some things, but whoever reads it must be convinced of the reality of the writing, grim, sordid and repulsive though the facts disclosed may be. It was due to the interest in this budding author which Miss Mary L. Pendered took that he was put in touch with a famous house of publishers, and we have little doubt that there will be no lack of sensible people to read it. To every reader there will be conveyed the horror and futility of modern warfare, and the realisation of what depths to which mankind can be abased. Can any of us in our sane moments justify the brutality, the cruelty, and the ghoulish stories that are outlined? We of the older generation, who know by bitter experience what the last terrible war meant to many, have long come to a decision on our attitude towards war, but a good purpose will be served if, by means of books such as the one we have before us, it is brought home to the rising generation that war is one of the greatest plagues that can afflict humanity, and "a fearful thing e 'en in a righteous cause."
(*Wellingborough News*, May 1930.)

An Ex-Serviceman's Opinion of *Hell on Earth* Of war books there seems to be no end since "All Quiet on the Western Front" set the fashion for depicting the ghastliness of warfare in crude colours. Each fresh contribution to this war literature is heralded as something out of the ordinary rut, but too often they are found to be feeble imitations of "All Quiet" making up for their deficiencies with added coarseness.

Now comes a war book by a local man – Mr. F. Haydn Hornsey, of Wellingborough. By reason of it being written by somebody in our midst it will arouse great interest locally… Its local interest apart, what shall we say of its merit as a war chronicle? The publishers' note claims it as "something new in the seething whirlpool of war books," and for once I think we may allow the description to stand.

It is noteworthy in that it is the work of a man whose experience of warfare was confined to the final phases on the Western Front. It was April 1918 before he crossed the Channel, the reason being that he was too young to have gone before. It was in November, 1917, that he became eighteen. Thus he got to the front shortly after the Germans started their Big Push. There was no time for putting drafts through their paces in the Bull Ring in those momentous days, and almost at once this Northamptonshire lad found himself in the thick of things.

His experiences in the British retreat make up the greater portion of the record. The book has no pretensions to literary style, even grammatical deficiencies have been left untouched by the publishers. In this they did wisely, for to have "dressed up" this grim chronicle could only have resulted in marring its effectiveness which the feeling of actuality imparted by its uncouth style renders deadly. The writer tells us in his own words what happened to himself and his mates. His language is not always choice, but it is the authentic vocabulary of the troops. We see how young fellows torn by the stern needs of war from their peaceful avocations, reacted to the stimulus of bellicosity pumped into the men on military training grounds. Germans are continually referred to by an epithet which might well have been accorded the treatment meted out to other objectionable terms – represented by a dash – and we see them through vengeful eyes.

"...Not one prisoner did our battalion take – all were shot dead. What was the good of taking prisoners? They had to be fed. Who could bother to take them back to a prison camp... Shoot the ----- out of the way. That was the spirit."

I am thankful that it was a spirit of which I personally did not see much evidence. It is pleasant to find in the book unstinted admiration expressed of the action of a "Jerry" who ceased firing his machine gun to allow stretcher-bearers with a wounded man to get safely away.

Hell on Earth bears witness too, to the cheerfulness under privation which was a characteristic of the British Tommy, and there are humorous episodes which give relief to the sombreness of the narrative.

Brigadier-General Crozier has written a war book in which much prominence is given to wine and women. "He who hopes to wage war without wine and women is living in a fool's paradise," says the gallant General. Other war books have been equally outspoken on this subject, and it will be naturally wondered what the one before us has to say. It may be said at once that so far as wine is concerned it is no exception and the fact that women play a less conspicuous part may be attributed to the circumstances. Obviously when an Army is fighting "with its back to the wall" there is no time for amatory episodes. Even so we do not escape the subject altogether. The draft in which the writer went out was but a few hours in Calais, but those few hours were long enough for a visit to be paid to "No.11." Personally, I think the story would not have lost anything by the omission of the chapter recording this incident.

To sum up, this stark narrative succeeds despite the writer's limited vocabulary in giving a vivid picture of a soldier's experience during the retreat of 1918, and disclosing as it does the horrors of modern warfare, the book is a valuable peace propaganda...

A record of absorbing interest and truth... I prophesy that this opinion will be shared by the majority of readers of "Hell on Earth." (***Northamptonshire Advertiser*, May 1930.)**

Fig. 3 Frank Haydn Hornsey on active service. France, May 1918

After the Great War, F. Haydn Hornsey worked as an insurance agent for the Pearl Assurance Company, based around the Wellingborough area. He continued working for the Pearl until his retirement.

On 28th April 1921 F. Haydn Hornsey was married to Zana Alison West at Finedon Parish Church. They had two daughters, Eileen and Hazel. The family moved to Ivy House, Doddington Road, Earls Barton, in the early 1930s. After the death of Zana in 1956, Haydn married Molly Sandall.

In the years following the Great War, F. Haydn Hornsey became an accomplished and well respected angler, winning many coarse fishing competitions in the Northamptonshire area. He regularly contributed articles to the *Northamptonshire Advertiser*, writing the Angling Column for 27 years. He also wrote articles for the *Angling Times*. F. Haydn Hornsey had a second book published in 1951 by Herbert Jenkins (London). The title of this popular book was *Match Fishing with the Champions*.

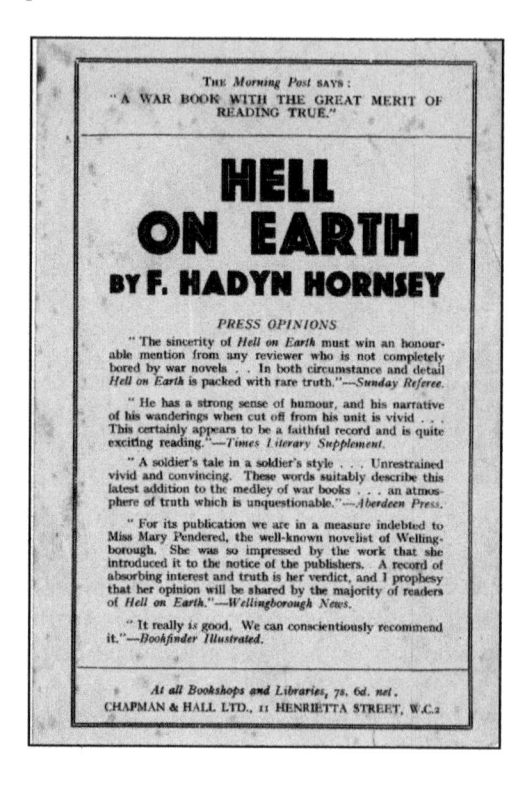

Fig. 4 Advert for Hell on Earth 1930

CONCLUSIONS

How accurate is the book? F. Haydn Hornsey kept a Boots Pocket Diary (Fig 2), and this formed the skeleton around which he wrote his book *Hell on Earth*. After checking the diary against the 11th (Service) Battalion, Suffolk Regiment (Cambridgeshire) War Diary and the history of the 34th Division, the brief diary commentary seems to be remarkably accurate, even though it must have been difficult to write entries during the momentous events of the retreat in April 1918.

It is clear that the story told in this book fits well into the historical context, and, as was claimed in the book reviews of 1930, it is largely based on facts. It is useful to compare one incident in the book with a section of the Battalion War Diary in order to illustrate this.

> ***Hell on Earth* p. 110** At 9.30 the whole Battalion was on parade… The Commanding Officer fronted us saying, "Battalion, today is a proud day for us all. I have a certain number of awards. The medals have been won in the last rearguard action in which we have been fighting… I will now award the medals"
> "Myself I have won the D.S.O, Major T. the M.C., Captain K. the D.S.O., Captain Brown the M.C. All the Sergeant Majors and Sergeants, a few Corporals and Lance Corporals and two Privates each received a medal – I believe the privates were Officers servants… To see medals being distributed in a wholesale manner such as they were doing rather riled us."
>
> **Battalion War Diary 8th June 1918** "Battalion Parade for G.O.C. 183rd Inf. Brigade…
> At the end of the month, the Battalion War Diary notes the Honours given to the Battalion:–
> Major Wright M.C., two Lieutenants won the M.C., three Sergeant Majors and one sergeant won the D.S.M., (the list continues, with Corporals and Lance Corporals winning Military Medals) Two privates were awarded medals, 226837

Private Mathews the D.C.M. and 12668 Private Butcher C. the M.M."

The two accounts fit together well.

A. D. Harvey has quoted parts of F. Haydn Hornsey's *Hell on Earth* in a chapter entitled 'Truth' He believes that Hornsey was one of the authors described by the military historian, Cyril Falls who,

> "…sat down to produce one (*All Quiet on the Western Front pub. Jan 1929*) in the same vein after watching Herr Remarque's sales go soaring into the hundreds of thousands."
> (1)

This may be true, and it is clear that a well known Wellingborough literary figure, Mary Pendered, encouraged him to write the book. The book had taken twelve months to complete and was therefore written mainly in 1929, since the draft was at the publisher, Chapman and Hall before March 1930. The contract for publication was signed on 15th March 1930.

After almost 80 years, the book reveals much about the morale, attitude and resilience of an eighteen year old Private under the intense stress of the Retreat of April 1918. It is hoped that the book, which has largely been forgotten, will be rediscovered and studied by a new generation of readers interested in the momentous days of 1918.

NOTES ON THE BATTLES OF THE LYS, 9TH – 29TH APRIL 1918

The period of these battles forms the core of the early chapters in *Hell on Earth*. It is hoped that these notes will be helpful.

On the 9th April, the German Lys Offensive, codenamed 'Georgette' began. The German 6th Army attacked between Armentières and

Givenchy, pushing in a north-westerly direction towards the important railway centre of Hazebrook behind the junction of the British First and Second Armies. On 10th April, the German Fourth Army successfully attacked Messines village and some of the Messines - Wytchaete Ridge further to the north. Armentières lay directly between the converging German attacks.

The 11th (Service) Battalion Suffolk Regiment (Cambridgeshire) was part of the 34th Infantry Division. This Battalion, along with the 15th and 16th Battalions of the Royal Scots, formed the 101st Brigade. The commanding officer of the 34th Division was Major-General C. Lothian Nicholson, and his Divisional H.Q. was at Steenwerck. The 34th Divisional History notes that:–

> "The gaps in our ranks caused by the fighting on the 21/23rd March, had been filled up, but there had been no time to test or train the drafts, for the two Brigades were fully employed repairing and strengthening defences… As our infantry had lost 87 officers and 2,654 other ranks, the battalions were largely composed of these new drafts." (**2**)

F. Haydn Hornsey was one of these new drafts.

On 9th April 918, on the first day of the German 'Georgette' attack, the 101st Brigade was in reserve, and the 11th Suffolks were in the Erquinghem area, approximately one mile to the west of Armentières. F. Haydn Hornsey arrived on the evening of the 8th April as the area was being shelled by German artillery. The German artillery had opened up at 4.15 am:–

> "The volume of sound was so great that it could only portend an attack on a considerable scale, and as the hours passed and there was no cessation in the din, we all realised that yet another "day" had arrived, and all units and parties "stood to." The bombardment did not affect our front line, but our back

areas got more than usual shelling, Erquinghem especially being made almost untenable.(**2**)

The Battalion War Diary states that

"An attack was anticipated and Companies were got out in front of Erquinghem in trenches."

Conan Doyle, in his book *The British Campaign in Europe*, recounts that on the 9th April, the 101st Brigade was ordered to take position to cover the important bridge over the River Lys at Bac St. Maur. He tells us that the 11th Suffolks made their way into Fleurbaix and linked up with the 12th Suffolks of the 40th Division.

"These two sturdy East Anglian units held the village (Fleurbaix) in a very desperate fight for many hours." (**3**)

It seems certain that this is incorrect, as the 11th Suffolks was immersed in heavy fighting in front of Erquinghem on both the 9th and the 10th April, and was in no position to be able to move towards Fleurbaix. Doyle may well be referring to a Divisional order which could not be acted upon owing to the desperate circumstances caused by the German attack. This is confirmed in the 34th Divisional History, which informs us that the 12th Suffolks retreated northwards from the Fleurbaix area until they found themselves on the right side of the 11th Suffolks, and to the left of the Royal Scots, in front of Erquinghem.

The situation becomes clearer when one reads the *History of the 1/4th Battalion Duke of Wellington's (West Riding) Regiment* (**5**). Fig. 5 shows a map from this history and shows the situation on the 10th and 11th April. The position of the 11th Suffolks is where the Battalion War Diary indicated, in front of Erquinghem. The 1/4th Bn. Duke of Wellington's Regiment had been placed at the disposal of the 101st Infantry Brigade (34th Division), and was to close a gap where the

Germans had penetrated between the 16th Bn. Royal Scots on the right and the 11th Suffolks on its left.

By 10.00 am, the Dukes were moving forward through heavy shellfire to cross the River Lys to attempt to form a line with the 11th Suffolks. The main bridge was destroyed, but they managed to cross by means of a badly damaged bridge (where they crossed in single file) and by a wooden bridge near the church. Contact was made with the 11th Suffolks, but there was no sign of the Royal Scots. As a result, Erquinghem was now threatened from both the West and the South.

> "Late in the morning, an officer of the 11th Battalion Suffolk Regiment asked for reinforcements to close a gap in the line near the Rue du Moulin. In response, 'A' Company sent up a platoon... this Platoon was never seen again... Its fate remained a mystery until after the Armistice. Then, returned prisoners told how it had been surrounded by the enemy, and, after suffering heavily, the few survivors had been captured... About the middle of the afternoon the men of the 11th Battalion Suffolk Regiment who had been on the left of 'C' Company all day, withdrew, having their written orders to do so." (3)

[*Private A. Poulter of the Duke of Wellington's Regiment, earned the Victoria Cross in this action, for conspicuous bravery when acting as a stretcher-bearer.*]

At about 3.00 pm on 10th April, at 34th Divisional H.Q., it became clear that the 34th Division had become outflanked by the German advance and Major-General Nicholson ordered the retirement north of the River Lys. Haydn notes in his diary that the Armentières Bridge was blown up at 2.30pm and the Battalion War Diary states that the 11th Suffolks withdrew north of the River Lys at 5.00 pm. From this information it can be construed that when the remnants of the 11th Suffolks were ordered to withdraw, they crossed the River Lys at Erquinghem. Haydn writes of swimming across!

Fig. 5

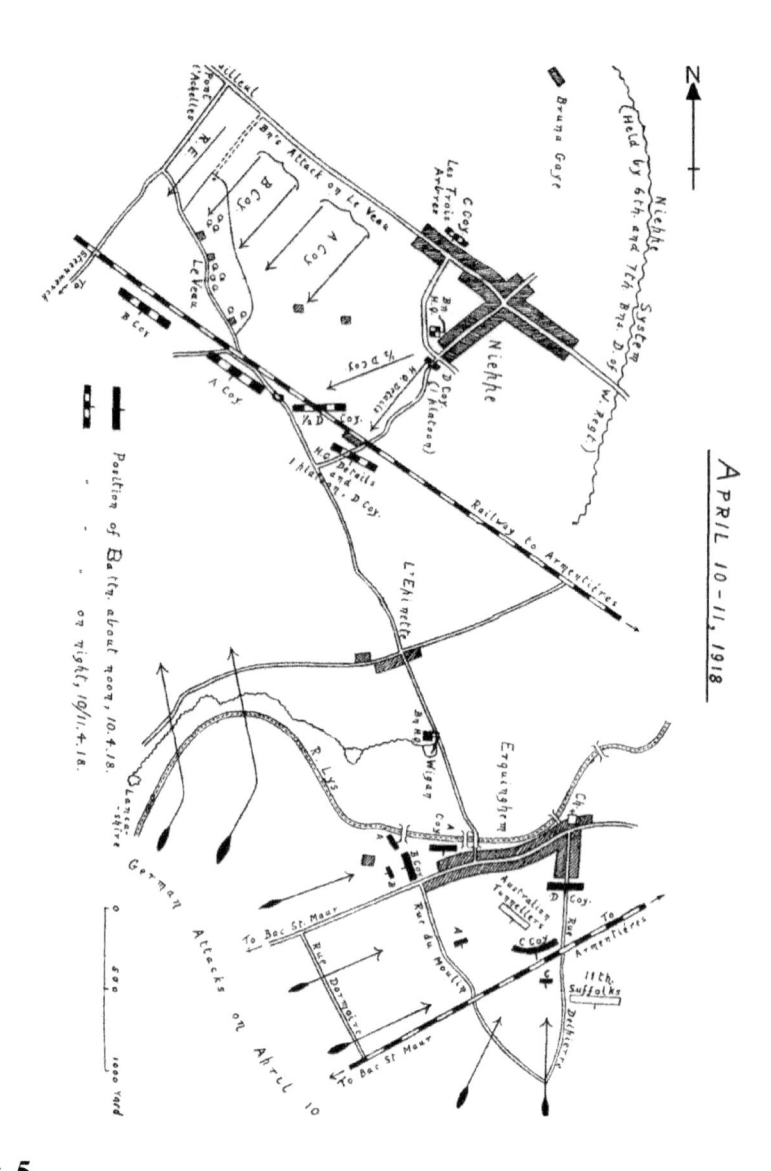

(From The History of the 1/4th Battalion Duke of Wellington's Regt.)

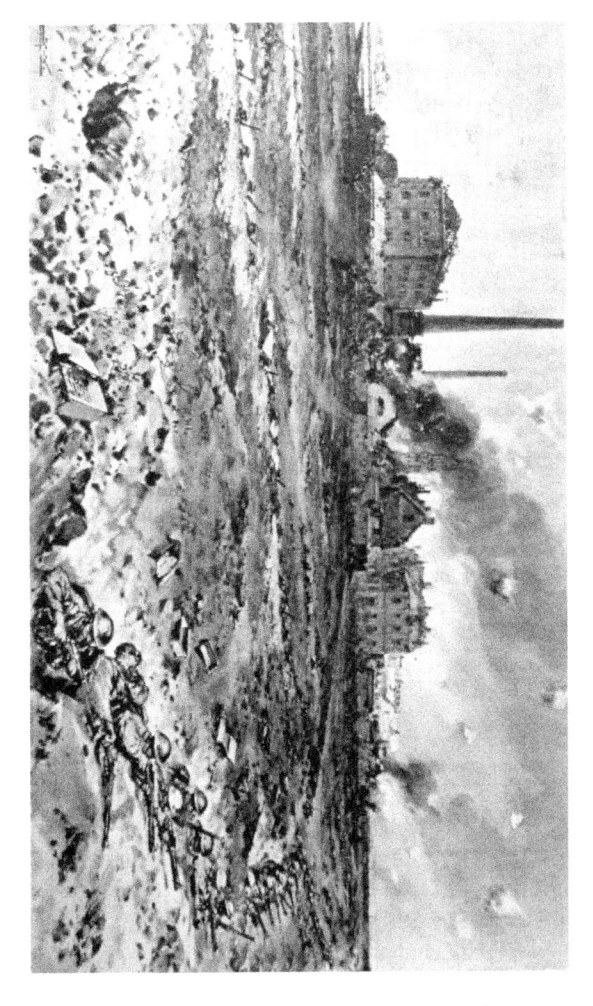

British frontline, Erquinghem (April 10th 1918)

(A sketch printed in The Illustrated London News April 27th 1918)

Other units of the 34th Division retreated through Armentières:–

> "…The town gradually became an irregular salient outflanked to a depth of three miles on the Plugstreet side and nearly seven miles in the direction of Bac St Maur. The salient was about four miles across. In this cauldron the 34th Division was exposed to anything the enemy cared to fire in its direction but was not assaulted frontally. The commander of the 34th Division, Major-General C. L .Nicholson, had suggested as early as the previous day that a retirement might be started rather than allow his division to be surrounded by default but he did not get the order until 1000 hours the following morning. Wearily the garrison slouched back through the deserted streets, still spattered with yellow stains from the gas bombardment; they straggled across the main square with its handful of trees still holding up splintered branches, past the twisted gas lamps and down the main road towards the Pont de Nieppe, the main bridge out of town. Units of the 40th Division, also penned in the salient made their way back over a railway bridge after the commanders of four battalions had conferred." (4)

The retirement had been covered on the right flank by the 1/4th Battalion of the Duke of Wellington's Regiment, part of the 147th Brigade. Conan Doyle writes:–

> "The 34th drew off in fine order, the rearguards stopping from time to time, especially in the streets of Armentières, for the purpose of beating back German patrols. All bridges were destroyed, and no unwounded prisoners left. The men of the 34th were loud in their praise of the way in which the Yorkshire Territorials of the 147th Brigade covered their right flank during this difficult and dangerous extraction." (3)

On 11th April, further retirement became imperative, fighting back all the way whilst under constant shellfire. By the next day, 12th April, the line had been pushed further back to De Seule. General Gore, the C.O. of the 101st Brigade was killed by shellfire during this retreat.

[*On 11th April a cousin of Haydn, Frederick A. Hornsey was killed on Messines Ridge. He was 17 years old and was serving with the 2nd Regiment South African Infantry (and had been wounded in September 1917). Prior to leaving for France, Haydn and Frederick had met in Wellingborough whilst both were on leave. Frederick Hornsey's name is on The Menin Gate Memorial to the Missing.*]

The heavy fighting continued, with the 11th Suffolks slowly being pushed back, to Bailleul town on the 14th April, then to the railway line S.E. of Bailleul Station on the 15th April. On the 16th April, the remains of the 34th Division formed a new line near St. Jans Cappel, which held firm.

> "On April 17th there was yet another day of heavy fighting upon this line... but the position was successfully held, and one more limit seemed to have been reached in the advance. The same six Brigades under General Nicholson, reduced now to the strength of Battalions, were still throwing an iron bar across the German path. From the right the 147th, 74th, 101st, 102nd, 103rd, and 88th, all of them with set teeth, held on to the appointed line which receded under pressure and was yet again re-established." **(2)**

Late on 20th April, the 11th Suffolks were relieved by the French and the Battalion's part in the Battle of the Lys came to an end.

The Battalion War Diary lists the following casualties during the month of April 1918:-

Killed	Officers	4	Other ranks	39
Died of wounds	Officers	4	Other ranks	3
Wounded	Officers	10	Other ranks	157
Missing	Officers	5	Other ranks	272

(The figures given in the CD *Soldiers Died in the Great War* for April 1918, are Officers killed 8 and Other Ranks killed 120.)

F. Haydn Hornsey had been listed as one of the missing during the retreat, and in *Hell on Earth* (p. 105) he writes about his eventual return to his Battalion.

> "At last we arrived at the camp… Although with our own Battalion there was not one chap amongst them with whom we came out – this was easily explained, the battalion had been made up with new troops to full strength – there is no doubt that it was needed, for out of 1,200 men who went into that wheat field on the 7th April, less than 50 answered the roll call when they were taken out of action a few days after – 'C' company was completely wiped out and I believe we three were the only survivors."

WITH THE 61ST DIVISION MAY – OCTOBER 1918

On 25th May, orders were received that the 11th Suffolk Battalion was to leave the 34th Division and join the 61st (2nd South Midland) Division. The Battalion then spent about 10 weeks in the neighbourhood of St Floris. During this period, F. Haydn Hornsey was sent on a course at the Aire sur Lys Sniper School (p.137 *Hell on Earth*). In his Pocket Diary he notes the date as 13th June, arriving at midnight. By 7th August, the Battalion was involved in fighting around Merville and this continued until 1st September when they were withdrawn to divisional reserve for a few days.

xviii

Haydn's active service came to an end in August 1918, when he was gassed and, according to his account in "Hell on Earth", taken to a Field Hospital near to Le Havre (p.176 *Hell on Earth*). The Battalion War Diary states that during August 1918, 230 Officers and Other Ranks were gassed or wounded. The Regimental History records that on August 19th the Battalion was in the Merville area when the Germans evacuated the town.

> "The 11th Battalion closely followed the enemy and harassed them as much as possible. On the 20th August, a day of patrol encounters, the advance was resumed and a new line established by the 11th Battalion. This new line was subjected to heavy artillery fire for over an hour at about midnight. In the morning the battalion acted as the advance guard for the brigade; one company, along with part of another, was caught in a heavy gas-shell (Yellow Cross) and HE barrage, suffering heavy casualties"**(6).**

It is probable that Haydn was one of these casualties, since there is an entry in the Northampton Evening Telegraph relating that Haydn had been gassed in August.

Northamptonshire Evening Telegraph   Mon. Oct. 28th 1918
Roll of Honour
Wellingborough soldier in Hospital

Pte. F.H.Hornsey of the Cambs Regt. and son of Mr. F. Hornsey, of Cambridge Street, Wellingborough, is now in hospital, suffering from trench fever. He has been in France for about eight months, and is 20 years of age. Before enlisting he worked on a farm at Cransley, and later with the late Mr. G. Day of Orlingbury. Private Hornsey was gassed in August of this year.

If Haydn had stayed with the 11th Suffolks for a few more weeks, he would have been involved in the re-capture of Erquinghem on the 11th September 1918, exactly five months after they had been driven out by the German "Georgette" attack.

POSTSCRIPT A– THE GERMAN VERSION OF *HELL ON EARTH*

In November 2004, an internet search showed that an antiquarian bookshop in Germany had a copy of *Hell on Earth*. The description of this book did not match the Chapman and Hall publication, since the title was different:–

> "Hell on Earth. A Personal Record of the Battle of the Lys April 1918" **(7)**

It had been published in Germany by B. G. Teubner. The date of publication was 1935, some five years after the Chapman and Hall publication. (Fig. 6 & 7)

The book is a paperback with just 60 pages (the original book has 244 pages). It is an abridged extract taken from the 1930 book *Hell on Earth*. The abridged text is taken from the sections covering the Battle of the River Lys. Only minor changes have been made to the text, and it is written in English. The introduction is in German and there is a German vocabulary and glossary at the back of the book (pp. 49 – 60).

Fig. 6 Teubner Publication 1935

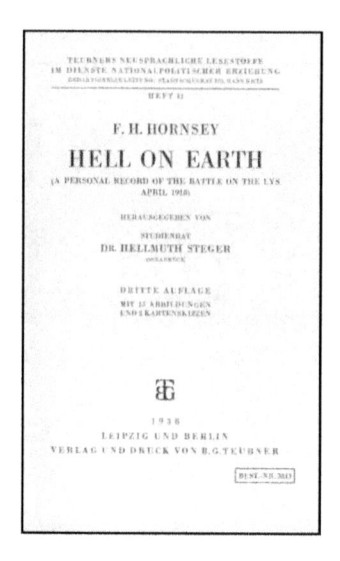

Fig. 7 Teubner Publication - Title Page

This book has 2 maps and fifteen photographs, whereas the original (Chapman and Hall, 1930) publication has none.

Surviving relatives of F. Haydn Hornsey had no knowledge of the existence of this book, and they are certain that F. Haydn Hornsey was completely unaware of the abridged German version.

The book was used as an educational text book in Germany. It has been established that further editions were published in 1936, 1937, and 1938. There is a preface, printed in German, on the inside of the front cover. The Preface explains why the book has been published, and sets the context of the book. It is one of a series of texts published by Teubner where the subject matter concerns the ordinary, poorly educated British worker (*see* The Introduction Fig 8).

> With this new edition, a direction is being followed which the publisher has already pursued in its foreign language literature. As is the case in the book *No Hands Wanted*, where a man of the people has his say about his fate due to unemployment (first edition in Germany!), in this publication also, "an illiterate man," recounts in accordance with the facts what he experienced in the "Battle of the Lys" – the second biggest breakthrough offensive in Flanders (April 1918). "He gives a very lively and impressive account of the fury and rapidity of the German advance simply by telling things how they were", as the publisher tells us in the foreword of the original English edition.
>
> Having landed in Calais one day, being taken by train to the front the next day, and a day later being involved in "one of the heaviest and most formidable battles of world history" the military career of F. H. Hornsey begins. To take us up to this moment, the following short excerpts are presented from his narration. Hornsey belonged to a reserve troop of approximately one hundred men, who, after disembarking marched to join its regiment at the front to occupy a reserve position in the Armentières section, approximately 5 Km behind the front line. Kilometre after kilometre are traversed, some of them utterly futile as the road they follow is continually wrong. The shelling of the front gets nearer and nearer, darkness interrupts, they are nearer to their destination – but where the front line is nobody knows. Fatigue and hunger exhaust the powers of the young team – not yet used to long marches with full kit. After the regiment is finally found and the replacements are divided up, the disappointment sets in: "When we enquired about food the Sergeant Major said rations for to-morrow had been distributed and he could get no more to-night." But sleep also gives no respite, as shortly before midnight the German bombardment of the troops' position with gas shells begins. This is where Hornsey's narration starts, as he acquaints us with the battle in which Marshall Haig's battle decree was made famous "*With our backs to the wall*, - - - each one of us must fight on to the end."

Fig. 8 Teubner Introductory Text (Translation from German)

Alterations have been made to the original text and these changes seem to involve removing some negative comments which had been made referring to German soldiers.

The Teubner version of the book was probably an attempt by the National Socialists to glorify the German achievements in the Battle of the River Lys and to show that the working class Englishman was not the enemy of Germany. It also attempts to show that the ordinary British soldier admired the strength and fighting qualities of the German soldier. The dates of publication, between 1935 and 1938, seem to strengthen this hypothesis.

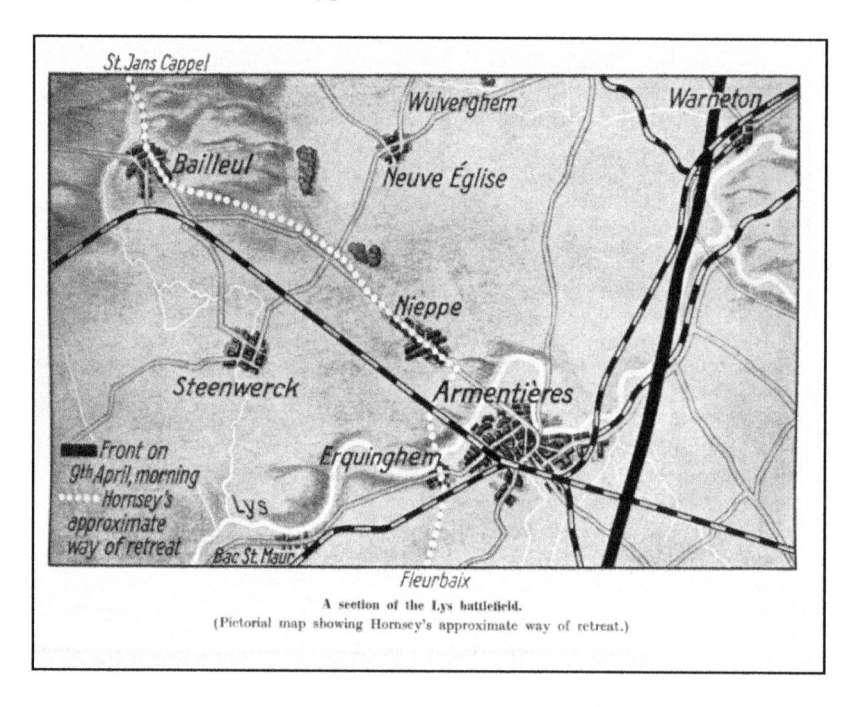

A section of the Lys battlefield.
(Pictorial map showing Hornsey's approximate way of retreat.)

Fig. 9 F. Haydn Hornsey's Approximate Line of Retreat. (from the Teubner Publication)

In 1953, the Teubner version of *Hell on Earth* was still on the list of literature which could be selected for use in educational establishments in the German Democratic Republic. This list was published by the Ministry for National Education of the GDR (Third Supplement 1953, entry number 2160).

In 1980, John Tolland, in his book, *No Man's Land* quotes extensively from the Teubner version of *Hell on Earth* to give first hand factual accounts on the Battle of the Lys. (**8**)

The German version poses a number of questions. Did Chapman and Hall give permission for the abridged version? Could it be that in pre-war Germany, more people had read F. H. Hornsey's account of his Great War experiences than had read it in Britain?

POSTSCRIPT B

The Welsh Language Novel   "GWAED GWIRION"

In 2014 new information came to light with regard to a Welsh language book entitled **Gwaed Gwirion**. This novel had been written in 1965 by Emyr Jones, and has become a classic in the Welsh language.

Prior to researching for a reprint by Gomer press in 2014, Professor Gerwyn Williams made an important discovery.

Parts of the book had been taken from Hell on Earth and translated into Welsh. There was no attribution in the novel of F. Haydn Hornsey or Hell on Earth. The 2014 reprint (**9**) now has acknowledged the part which F. Haydn Hornsey unknowingly played in Gwaed Gwirion. (See Fig. 10.) As with the Teubner version, there was no knowledge of the existence of this book within the family and it is certain that F. Haydn Hornsey was completely unaware of it.

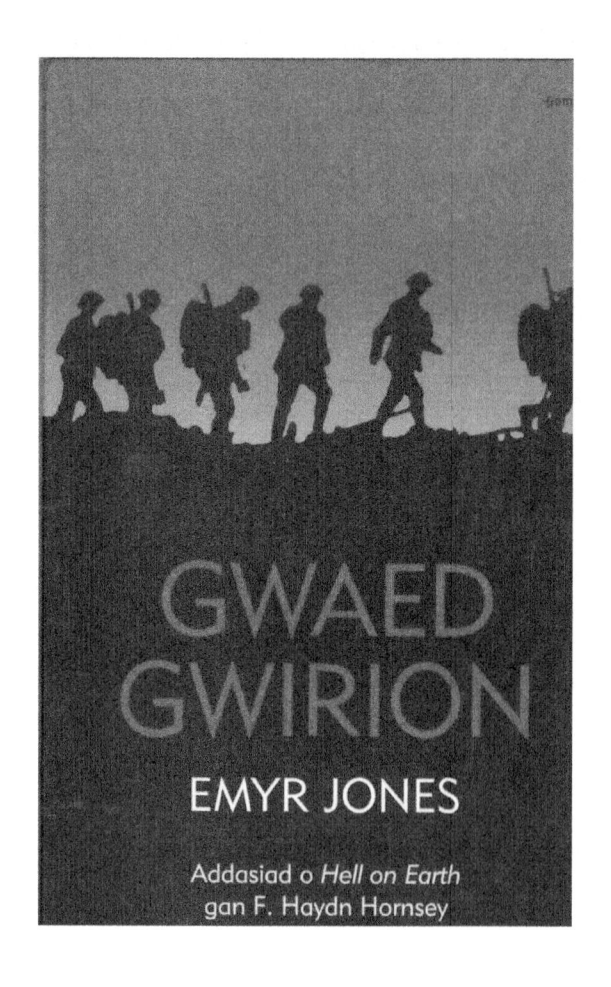

Fig. 10 Welsh language novel Gwaed Gwirion (Gomer Press 2014)

REFERENCES

The War Diary of the 11th (Service) Battalion Suffolk Regiment (Cambridgeshire). Public Record Office Ref. WO 95/2458.

(**1**) *A Muse of Fire. Literature, Art and War*. A. D. Harvey (The Hambledon Press 1998), pp.140, 158-159

(**2**) *The 34th Division 1915 - 1919*. Lieut. Colonel J. Shakespear. (The Naval & Military Press)

(**3**) *The British Campaigns in Europe 1914 - 1918*. Arthur Conan Doyle (Geoffrey Bles).

(**4**) *See How They Ran. The British Retreat of 1918*. William Moore. (Sphere)

(**5**) *The History of the 1/4th Battalion Duke of Wellington's (West Riding) Regiment 1914 - 1919*. P. Bales (Edward Mortimer)

(**6**) *The History of the Suffolk Regiment 1914-1927*. Lieut. - Colonel C. C. R. Murphy. (Hutchinson & Co.)

(**7**) *Hell on Earth (A personal Record of the Battle on the Lys April 1918)*. F. H. Hornsey. Herausgegeben von Dr.Helmuth Steger. (B. G. Teubner Leipzig und Berlin 1935)

(**8**) *No Man's Land*. John Tolland (Smithmark 1995), pp.149, 160,165, 169 – 170

(**9**) *Gwaed Gwirion*. Emyr Jones & F H Hornsey (Gomer Press 2014)

Acknowledgements

Thanks to T. Croucher and J. A. Richardson for their invaluable help and advice.

To M. J. Richardson for translating the German introduction in the Teubner publication.

Also thanks to Elinor and all at Gomer Press for keeping me informed of developments with the re-publication of Gwaed Gwirion in 2014.

R S Richardson   Conistone-with-Kilnsey   2017

HELL ON EARTH

F. HAYDN HORNSEY

First Published Chapman & Hall, 11 Henrietta Street, London, W.C.2, 1930

Kindle E Book Edition   R. S. Richardson 2014

Paperback edition with new introduction R S Richardson   2017

PUBLISHER'S NOTE *(From 1930 Edition)*

THE manuscript of this book was sent to us by the advice of Miss Mary L. Pendered, the well-known novelist, who had read it, and pronounced it a record of absorbing interest and obvious truth. That opinion will, we believe, be shared by most of its readers, especially when the circumstances of its production are taken into consideration.

The author, who lives in a Midland town, enlisted under the Conscription Act, immediately after his eighteenth birthday, and went over to France in April, 1918, just after the big German offensive. His regiment was sent to a spot where the British line had been broken, and soon they were in retreat. His record, which is pure fact from start to finish, has been printed exactly as he wrote it. No attempt has been made to improve the style, or even to correct errors in grammar. For the outstanding value of the document lies in its actuality; and, in the simple qualities of sincerity and force, this true tale seems to its publishers to bear comparison with any of the war records which have appeared in such numbers during the last few months

ARTHUR WAUGH

Table of Contents

CHAPTER I	I LEAVE MY HOME TO ENLIST	1
CHAPTER II	OFF TO FRANCE	7
CHAPTER III	CALAIS. THE HOUSE WITH THE RED LAMP	10
CHAPTER IV	WE GO TO THE WESTERN FRONT	12
CHAPTER V	THE ENEMY ATTACK	14
CHAPTER VI	OUR RETREAT CONTINUES	21
CHAPTER VII	LOST IN FRANCE	37
CHAPTER VIII	A NIGHT AT THE FARM	54
CHAPTER IX	BILL'S PICNIC AT BAILLEUL	72
CHAPTER X	THE GOLDEN CROSS	86
CHAPTER XI	WE REJOIN OUR REGIMENT	100
CHAPTER XII	AT REST IN THE SOUTH OF FRANCE	114
CHAPTER XIII	DOWN YPRES WAY	119
CHAPTER XIV	THE RAID AT LONE TREE POST	125
CHAPTER XV	AN OBSERVATION POST	137
CHAPTER XVI	THE ALLIES ATTACK	146
CHAPTER XVII	A NIGHT OF HORRORS	152
CHAPTER XVIII	THE PILL BOX	164
CHAPTER XIX	LUCK DESERTS US	169

HELL ON EARTH

CHAPTER I

I LEAVE MY HOME TO ENLIST

WHO could say what might be the future of just one more young man who stood waiting his turn in the Barracks of his County Town to enlist early one November morning in 1917?

I was just one more of thousands who had reached 18 years of age, and had to enlist under the Conscription Act. I was fair haired, tall, strong and well built, and a picture of health – as is usual when following an outdoor occupation. A few brief minutes in the Medical Officer's room was sufficient to pass me A1. Half an hour later I was in an ill fitting suit of khaki. It was made to fit later with the aid of a needle and thread, a kit bag with spare suit and other items which help to make a soldier's outfit complete, and still later I was marched down the street to the station armed with a Railway Warrant – booked to a training Camp on the East coast. Not that I really minded joining. I was convinced what thousands of others had done and were still doing – I could do. I arrived at my destination.

The Railway station was alive with 'Red Caps' (Military Police) who pounced on me to see my papers, and their chief characteristic was that they appeared to glorify in showing their Authority. About an hour later I was placed in a line Regiment with a number of five figures, and of course the usual rank of 'Private' Fred

Smith. Soon the training commenced – up in the morning at 6.30 – Physical Jerks or perhaps Coal fatigue, then drill, drill, drill – nothing but drill or guards, bullied and swore at by Sergeants and Sergeant Majors until I did realize there was a difference between civil life and the life of a private in training for the front. Often I stood in concrete trenches on the sea front until long past midnight with full fighting kit on – awaiting the invading enemy. Other nights they sent us into the fields, bombing or putting up barbwire entanglements in the dark. Our kit and uniforms of course got muddy and wet but we had to be spick and span on parade early next morning and God help the one whom the Sergeant Major spotted with dirty boots or who wanted a shave, or whose buttons were not bright. How he used to catch hold of our ears and pull us forward, raving and swearing what he would do with us and what he would not!

"Liven your ideas up my lad, you dirty Sod. Don't answer me back! If you broke your mother's heart you won't break mine! – stand still damn you. Report at the cookhouse to-night at 5.30 and I'll find you a job." And so on and on as the weary days dragged by.

We went to the cookhouse, and a little Lance-Corporal ordered us to start cleaning several hundredweights of potatoes – and he kindly let us know that when we had done that there was plenty of coal to fetch up from the Dump. I might say that the dump was quite a quarter of a mile away!

As we sat outside the cookhouse on a box scrubbing the potatoes that cold November night my thoughts wandered and I guessed what I should be doing if things had been different and there was no War. How far that life seemed away already. Day by day it seemed to get farther and farther away and many things I used to love seemed now only a dream.

Christmas came and we got four days leave. Home for four days; breakfast in bed; a score of friends to see; my best girl to give a whirlwind visit; to Dances and the Pictures; and before I knew where I was I had arrived back with my unit.

My pal was Bill Worthy, and, like me, he was an outdoor worker but he was dark and of shorter stature. A Londoner with a cockney accent, good natured, but easy going, thinking only of to-day and never of the morrow, and a born gambler. Gambling was his chief pastime.

His Christmas leave ended with a night in the Guard Room for staying longer than he was entitled to do. The following morning he was brought before the Commanding Officer and received fourteen days confinement to barracks and pay stopped for a corresponding period. These sort of things did not worry Bill in the least. What was 14 days C.B. and 14 days' pay stopped when he had two whole extra days with his pals in London – only two things seemed to worry Bill – how to get rid of the money when he drew it on a Friday and his rheumatic knee.

All punishment must come to an end sometime if you can only stand it. It nearly killed Bill to stay in at night after parades were done. How many 'Subs' he had from his Pals to tide him over that fortnight I never shall know! Anyhow after many scrapes and punishments by Sergeant Major Lane we arrive to March 1st, 1918.

Nearly full blown soldiers ready for the front, all passed out in rifle shooting and drill, besides having knowledge in firing the Lewis Gun and throwing all sorts of Bombs – it was really amazing how quickly they produced the goods in those days.

Then came our final leave – Seven days draught leave before we went to the front. How those seven days flew! But what a royal time we had! Who cared? Who knew if ever we should see our dear home town again and all those who were dear to us? On with the dance, on with the joy-rides, let the wine flow freely – who cared for the Sergeant Major? Due back to-morrow.

What a night that last night! How many promises were made it would be hard to say but how many would be kept would be easier to answer. Cissy said I must go back in the morning.

"Whatever happens you do not want them to fetch you, do you?" she cried, and then after many farewells and promises I said I would go back in the morning. But of course I had no intentions of going. I had decided to have two extra days like Bill did, and blast the Sergeant Major and the whole Army if it came to that – who cared for anybody when you were booked for the front? They did not trouble to fetch you until you had been over your time about four days.

Imagine Cissy's surprise when I turned up outside where she worked and told her I had decided to stay two more days. Her face went white – then red. She was just as excited as I and just as pleased that I was staying. Then more arrangements were to be made, but like all good things, the end must come and bring the price.

A night in the Guard Room, then brought up in front of the Company Officer for sentence. Twenty eight days' pay stopped.

Hurray! Got off light. What was 28 days' pay? It was only entered up in your pay book and your account would be squared at the end of the War – if ever it did stop. The Sergeant marched me back by myself to my Company and handed me over.

I found out after the Parade Bill had stayed over one day extra and got twenty one days' pay stopped – so I consider myself fortunate with my punishment!

One day followed another very much alike until March slipped out. All this time we were under orders for the front – each afternoon we expected orders to "hand in our bed." The draughts usually left at night. In this centre thousands of troops were under orders and no one seemed to know where we were going. All sorts of rumours were flying about. I had not the slightest doubt it would he France – and France it was. We had our Orders on April 4th. I sent a wire home to let my folks know and a letter would follow.

What a funny feeling I had. Certainly not fright – far from it, but when I knew where I had to go to, it was a feeling of great excitement and expectancy. The call of youth for adventure – the same call that our forefathers have had for generations – believe me, then I was looking forward to it – anxious to get at it. Thoughts of danger never entered my head. Little did I dream what I was to go through in the course of the next few weeks. I wonder if the same feelings would have been there had I known?

Excitement reigned supreme. Thousands were packing up that day and making final arrangements – the youth of England – they were all 18 and 19 years old, the last flower of England's manhood. Many, a few weeks ago still apprenticed in one trade or another, many more were just from school. These were the men proceeding to France to fill the gaps.

These men – or shall we say boys? were to be flung straight into the fury of battle in an endeavour to turn the tide of Germany's Great Offensive! For weeks the British Headquarters knew she was going to attack – knew nearly to the day, to the Secter.

All were light hearted. Glancing at the faces and hearing the jokes one would have thought we were going to a football match, or, as Bill put it, "a blinkin' picnic." What a race of people are the English!

Just a final visit to the Medical Officer. We then proceeded to draw our overseas equipment, a pay book, and, worst job of all, parting with our straw bed and blankets. But at last we got this all over and we had the afternoon off. I went down to the town and bought a good supply of cigarettes and a few things that might be useful.

We were to parade at 7.30 so Bill and I went out for a good meal while we had the chance. Seven-thirty found us on the parade ground, with full marching orders, to answer the roll call. A few words from the Commanding Officer and then the band joined us. Martial music and a cheer from a few pals that were being left behind and we marched to the station. We were packed eight in a carriage and there was not much room to spare for our Kit and rifles. We realised the truth of the phrase "packed like sardines."

Now the worst part of the whole business – the parting. Fathers, Mothers, Sisters, Brothers, Sweethearts – many of them came to see us off. A terrible farewell! How brave were all those mothers! No one, but themselves really knew how they must have felt. No one was there that I knew thank goodness! I was pleased it was so.

Just before nine o'clock the long troop train began to move-the band played 'Good bye-e,' the train slowly drew out, and we were off.

CHAPTER II

OFF TO FRANCE

THE windows were packed with men waving good-bye. All tried to be cheerful, but how many broken hearts were left behind that night on the station platform I dare not think.

Most of the fellows were very quiet as the train got clear of the platform, but as we rattled on things began to look up and by the time London was reached everyone appeared in 'high jinks.' We reached London at 12.20, and slowly proceeded through the Metropolitan Area. As the train crawled along quite a number of men jumped out and deserted. Most of these men were Jews, many of them no doubt being conscripted from the London District. The temptation of being near home was too much for them, and I wondered what the fate of each might be when they were brought back again!

The train increased its speed to Dover and arrived at 3.20 on Friday morning. It was then as black as pitch and raining heavily. We marched up one of the stiffest hills I have ever experienced to what was called a 'rest camp.' Our beds were the bare boards! We had to lie down in our wet clothes and when I awoke from a doze about 5.45 I was shivering in every limb. We had breakfast of a sort and proceeded to the boat at 7.30, the sea then being very rough. An old Belgian boat was taking us over. We were packed on the Boat like herrings in a tin, and the spray dashed over the sides and soaked us to the skin. I already felt sick so I pushed myself through until I got to the outside. My rifle was red with rust from the sea water.

The troop ship was guarded by two destroyers – one on each side of her, but fate was kind and the journey was quiet. We arrived at Calais about 12 o'clock, but how cold and wet and shivering we all were! I felt sick, but it soon passed off when we were marching through Calais. What narrow streets and bad rough roads – all cobbles. That was my first impression of France. We marched about eight miles to one of the rest camps and distributing stations. Here thousands of soldiers lay for a few days until they were dispatched to their particular unit. Thousands of troops the last few days had been sent to one particular Sector. Headquarters knew that a German attack was now very near, as all the railways and roads leading to the battle front on the enemy side of the trenches had been packed with German troops, and, their big guns were coming up.

We were packed twenty in a tent absolutely like sardines in a tin. We got hold of some tea about 4 o'clock which was hot and greasy – that certainly was something to be thankful for.

I lost Bill for an hour after tea but he put in an appearance and said, "Broke already! And do you know the 'hook' hasn't come up the last eleven times! Lend me a dollar until I hear from home."

Bill had his usual daily flutter on the Crown and Anchor board and it did not matter to what part of the camp you went you could always see Crown and Anchor or some other gambling game in progress.

I of course lent Bill his dollar and we went back together to have another gamble.

Behind the third tent an old sweat (an old soldier) was running this game. About twenty of our 'Mob' were round him. Bill pushing his way to the front enquired if the 'hook' had come up during his absence. Poor Bill looked down his nose when told, "Sorry, old sporter, the 'hook' has just come up three times." Bill mumbled something about "just his luck" and if he only had a pound or two he would break him. "Come on my lad," said the old Soldier, "plonk your dough down thick and heavy, you come here in rags and go away in Motor Cars." Someone dropped on two francs. I was tempted to put two shillings on the heart, and Bill as usual commenced to back the 'hook.' No other part of the board worried him. Well it certainly did seem that he was lucky, for the 'hook' came up well for the next half hour, and then a 'Red Cap' came round the corner, and we all grabbed our money and bolted.

We dodged inside our tent and Bill had now twenty five francs compared with my eighteen. Some of the notes (all the winnings were in notes) were so dirty that it was difficult to distinguish them. Nearly all had gummed paper to keep them together.

Just when we were wondering what to do next pal Ben came in and wanted to make up a school of Solo. Of course Bill said, "Just the thing," and having no other interest at the moment consented. Soon one and others of us stood round the four playing and within a very few minutes of starting there were four times as many looking on and constantly giving advice. As we were not playing I was just about fed up with standing there when someone suggested going to Calais for an hour or two.

CHAPTER III

CALAIS – THE HOUSE WITH THE RED LAMP

IN a few minutes half a dozen of us were on the road outside the Camp waiting for a lorry. We did not have many minutes to wait and when one did come along, without asking the driver's consent, we all scrambled into the back and called out, "Are we right for Calais, mate?"

"Calais be damned. What the Hell do you think you are up to," the driver roared. "Get out, the whole b----- lot of you," and he brought the vehicle to a standstill.

We had no intention of getting out and the more the driver cursed the more we chaffed him. Someone asked him who owned the lorry. Did he or the British Government? If it belonged to the Army – well it belonged to us for we were the Army. I quite expected it would end in a free fight but after a heated argument and the exchange of some cigarettes he cooled down and consented to take us.

After a good bumpy ride we arrived at this town. Oh, what a night! I will leave you to guess whether it was by accident or design that we found ourselves in Number 11– one of the most notorious houses of ill fame in the town. Huge numbers of the British Army at one time or another had patronized inside its doors. We looked inside and received a very warm welcome as does everyone who visits these places.

One bottle of Vin Blonk and P. followed another. Everyone seemed happy. The place was thick with the haze of tobacco smoke and there was plenty of wine drinking. This house or 'Red Lamp' as it was better known by the troops, kept twenty girls. Some said it was allowed to be run under a licence granted by the French Government. Nobody appeared to know and nobody in our party cared.

The whole atmosphere was nauseous for what with the smell of smoke, the drink and the scent used by the French girls the place fairly 'hummed.' These girls were heavily powdered and painted, and were scantily clothed in thin flimsy dresses. They openly plied their questionable profession. Many of them were good looking with splendid figures – others looked worn and plainly showed signs of the wear and tear of their past life.

One of our party whose name was Sam sat with a pretty girl on his knees – they had just had another bottle of wine, but neither understood the language of each other. I heard him say, "Gawd blamey, my dear. I wish I was a bloomin' Froggy – I could then make you understand me. We could do with the whole bloomin' lot of yer in London at our little pub down 'Ammersmith way." Then the French girl would say, "La Angleterre Sol-dier tres bon, sol-dier promad, ah, oui."

Sam had drunk more wine than was good for him and got quite noisy. He suddenly disappeared but eventually turned up – poorer to the extent of four francs.

The end came all too quickly. We were all about broke and all had more drink than was good for us. No lorry came our way back, so a noisy party, singing, yelling and using all sorts of language staggered along the road towards camp – which was reached about midnight. We were soon challenged by a soldier on guard at the entrance to the camp, but luckily for us he was one of our fellows, so we got through alright. No doubt we should have 'clicked out' if he had belonged to another Regiment. Our tent was soon in an uproar – somebody trod on one of the fellow's feet. Sam, who was as drunk as a monkey forgot to take off his boots outside the tent and stepped on Bill's chest. Then of course there was a row. This was one of the pleasures of sleeping twenty in a tent.

CHAPTER IV

WE GO TO WESTERN FRONT

MORNING came at last! We paraded at 9.30 and were informed we were going to the 34th Division in the ____ Regiment. We were given rifle ammunition and ground sheets and told hourly to expect orders to go up, and on no account were we to leave Camp. Well the orders came through at last, so we marched right through Calais again and were loaded up in railway trucks. We travelled very slowly until we arrived at Steenwerch at 4 o'clock. We then marched about five miles and put up in an old cowshed with the roof half gone. The guns could easily be heard from here.

Early next morning about a hundred of us and an officer started for the front to join our unit – who were already up there somewhere. God knows how far we tramped – miles and miles. We continually lost our way. It would soon be night and still we had not found our unit. We were all fed up. The firing was nearer and then at last we arrived at the village where we expected to find our unit – only to discover that they had gone up the line somewhere that morning and no one knew where. Perhaps a few miles this side of Armentières, or on to the Erquingham road. We had just to keep going on – we had to find that unit for food.

Darkness came – things were getting bad and we had lost our way again. Thank God at last we arrived at Erquingham, where we were able to get a drink.

At Erquingham a large number of troops were massed. We enquired for our unit, "somewhere up this road" they thought we might find them. No one knew – no one cared. Only our party cared. There was nothing for us to do but keep going, and all this time we were carrying full packs. I was about done up. Bill was hobbling along – his knee had given out. How many miles we had come not one of us will ever know. We were reduced to a straggling mob.

"Have you seen anything of the ----- Regiment mate?" someone called out to a soldier who was going in the opposite direction.

"Yes," he said, "just round the corner." Thank God, that sounded better. We should soon be there. I was starving. Just round the corner proved to be about eight Kilometres on, but at last we found them. We were more dead than alive.

Our party was divided into four and sent to each Company. We were sent to 'C' Company.

We reported to the Sergeant Major. What a young man for a Sergeant Major! What a difference in appearance to the one we had just left behind in England! He took us into a 'tin bibby.' When we enquired about food he said rations for to-morrow were up and had been distributed. He said he could get no more to-night but might do so the following day. "The best thing I can advise you to do is to try and get some sleep," he said.

We were weary and hungry, and lying on the bare boards with our coats over us and our pack for a pillow, sleep would not come.

It was about 11.30 and a few Gas Shells were coming over from the German lines. The other chaps said the Germans shelled this part each night very badly. Cheerful, I must say! Oh, how hard were the boards we lay on, and how cold it was! My back felt as if it would break. How much I could eat now if I had the chance. The shelling grew heavy and many shells were dropping quite near. What a funny smell it was! Gas! We soon found out there was not sufficient to hurt – yet it was very unpleasant. A fellow said hundreds of soldiers were gassed last night at Erquingham. My tiredness was beginning to leave me – I really think I was just getting a little excited.

CHAPTER V

THE ENEMY ATTACK

IT was now well past midnight. Shells came faster and faster, and they were not all gas shells now. Many were dropping quite near. What a strange silence came over us! What was in store?

Crash!

A shell had dropped in the camp less than fifty yards away. Oh, the cruel noise! Shrapnel struck our tin hut with great force. I could hear men running about outside and cries of stretcher bearers, "For God's sake hurry."

Crash!

Another and another. What could we do? All of us were lying flat on the boards – our tiredness now forgotten, as also was our hunger. We were now in for it. Shells came faster and faster, but many were dropping short.

Crash!

That's another in the Camp. The left side of us this time. Many were hurt. Oh, the groans and cries of the wounded!

Just as the shelling was at its height and tension in our hut at breaking-point the Sergeant Major came inside (I noticed he had his tin hat on and revolver in his belt).

"Everybody get in fighting order quick. Get outside as soon as possible. All your pack leave in the hut," he shouted.

We were all outside in a few moments. Dawn was just breaking when we received orders to follow an officer. He led us through the camp to a large lorry which had brought a load of spades. Thousands of them. We all had to take one and then go up to an ammunition Dump where an extra three hundred rounds each were given us. Hand bombs were also dished out. He then led us into a large wheat field.

This part of the country was very flat. As far as the eye could see our fellows were digging in. Each one had to dig his own trench to protect himself. The enemy were shelling us like blazes but they were going well over. Several bursts of machine gun fire broke out – our Lewis Gunner fell dead, a bullet going through his heart. This fellow had come out with us and was killed but never saw a German. Such is mechanical War.

What was our position now? What had happened? What had become of our fellows who ought to be miles in front of us. The awful truth dawned upon me. The enemy had broken through all our lines and we were here to try and turn the tide. The shells were now falling nearer; our line was a great half-circle right across the country and we were about in the middle – another battalion on our left with Portuguese on our right.

The day broke out bright and sunny. I had dug three feet in when I struck water and was obliged to get out and dig on my knees and pack the clods of earth in front of my hole (that is all you could call it) for some sort of cover. The enemy moving about the skyline could easily be seen.

Captain Kay came along with his servant following.

"Do your best boys," he said. "The b----- have broke through, we have got to stop here as long as we can."

"Had no food to-day or yesterday? What do you mean? Can't help it. It's now too late to borrow any," he said when told that we had had no food for two days.

Machine gunning had commenced on both sides. The Captain carried along the line not appearing to notice that the machine gun bullets were flying all round him. His Servant went along more on his hands and knees than walking.

Captain Kay was an Englishman and a gentleman. He was more than brave. He was very often reckless with his bravery. He seemed to bear a charmed life for many times later have I seen him expose himself in front of the trenches and an enemy shot has been fired at him only to miss. He would not take the slightest notice of this and treated the German machine gun fire with contempt. He would say to his men, "You take cover." You can guess we all loved him, and there was not one of us who would not have followed him through Hell if he had only said the word.

Word now came along the line not to touch any water as it was all poisoned by the Gas which was continually coming over.

Shells were now breaking our frail line. The enemy had now got the range. A German Airplane was above us dropping lights for artillery range.

Where were our airmen? I never saw any that day. Were our guns all going back into safety? Great masses of German troops began to get near us taking all cover that was possible. Great hordes of his storm troops could be seen. He must have outnumbered us a Hundred to One. Our rifles and machine guns kept up a terrific fire and we gave him Hell. We were taking toll and a dreadful one, but still he came nearer and nearer. His machine guns were sweeping our posts.

It was now 10 o'clock in the morning. All our Officers were dead or wounded. The wounded could not be got away now that 'Jerry' was so near to us. Our only chance was to hang on until dark and trust to darkness to help us, but the odds looked too great. Already we had lost quite a lot of our men. Each hour the defenders were getting thinner and thinner. Our Lewis Guns were keeping up a steady fire. Another great fear was whether our ammunition would hang out until night.

Enemy Artillery was playing Hell with us. He had got the range well. Blast that airplane – here it is again! A machine gun was trained on it. The plane dropped more lights. Hundreds of rifles were turned on it. It did not look possible for it to escape from all that fire but it sailed safely back over the German lines and disappeared.

Some heavy shells were now dropping on our left. The German Artillery had now been on fourteen hours without ceasing, but of all the amazing things, as a lull came in the shell fire, I could hear a skylark singing beautifully. It sat on a clod of soil about thirty yards in front of me. It sat there singing – perhaps welcoming the approach of spring amidst all the noise and blood. How uncanny!

At 2.40 that afternoon the Germans attacked, they approached us under every bit of cover they could find supported by a terrific barrage of shell fire and machine guns – it was just as if Hell's gates were opened on to us. At 3 o'clock our right flank which had consisted of the Portuguese had gone – they bolted with very little resistance.

This terrific fight went on each minute, the Germans slowly and surely closing on us. At approximately 3.30 our left flank had gone. Harnessed now on three sides the German fire never ceasing – our fire getting weaker and weaker – how much longer? It was now a case of how many minutes. It was now or never. Several hundred of us jumped out of our holes and ran with our heads down fearing to look behind, running and praying that we could reach those farm ruins in time. A bullet hit my water bottle with great force. I really thought I had been hit.

"Why the Hell don't you hurry, Bill!" I yelled. He was about done up. Comrades were falling right and left. Still a hundred yards to go and bullets were as thick as ever. God, we reached the ruins, and as I reached them I had one glance back. Only a mere handful of us seemed to gain these buildings. The ground was littered with British dead and wounded.

What a sight these dead and wounded. The background swarming with Germans. His shell fire was as fierce as ever, his objective no doubt being the road along which we had got to go. Machine gun fire on three sides. I was faint. Bill seemed on the verge of despair. We were now going through the farm yard – a group of cattle stood there frightened and looking bewildered. Four or five more lay dead. I noticed a farm horse dead the other side of the yard, half blown away by shell fire.

Half a minute later we were going through the camp where we had slept the previous night. Everything was smashed to the ground – huts and tin bibby battered to the ground. Destruction on all sides. An officer lay dead here, no doubt killed in trying to get up to the lines in the early fighting.

We were making for the road as all the survivors were. That road lay to our freedom. We half ran, half walked down that road like madmen. Not an English shell was going over. Panic was everywhere. Our only thought was to escape this cruel fire.

At last we reached the road. Many dead and wounded lay here. A large shell had dropped right in the middle of the road tearing it to pieces. Some French refugees (consisting of father, mother and two young girls) were slowly walking down the road, the mother leading two cows and the man pushing a two wheeled conveyance with something covered over, and the two girls were carrying baskets and smaller bundles. Despair was written on their faces. The shells did not seem to worry them; misery was deeper in their hearts than all the damage the shells could now do. The shells had already done their worst to them. Their home lay in ruins – everything lost. They were simply going somewhere but to what place they did not know. They were taking a few things and a little food, and also their dead. The conveyance contained the dead body of their eldest daughter, killed by a shell that struck their home that morning.

We had got to keep on, yet the road was too dangerous for us to walk on. A dyke ran along the side of the road half full of water but that did not matter in the least. Straight in – anything was better than those bullets. Oh, my head was going round! I began to feel queer – was nearly done up – I began to have that don't care feeling come over me. I pulled myself together saying, ''No? It's no good giving way.'' We had got to go on.

"I don't want to die, keep on, keep on." That was my thought.

Slushing in the water. One minute up to your knees, and next up to your waist, but thank God we were getting away from those machine guns. On and on. Oh, how tired I was getting! In a flash my thoughts were of my home and my mother. I could see her smiling face, and she was saying, "Come on, come on, my boy."

"What the Hell's up with you, Fred?" said Bill.

"You've been standing like a b----- fool, do you want 'Jerry' to have us?"

The spell was broken and brought me back to earth. On and on, through water and mud.

As we got farther down the road, more and more troops joined us in that long dyke of freedom.

At last the village of Erquingham was reached – destruction everywhere – the same old tale. Ruin, desolation and death. Thousands and thousands of shells must have fallen in or around this village during the last twenty four hours. The street was ripped up and equipment of all sorts lay everywhere which had been discarded in the mad rush for liberty. The Estaminet at which we stopped the night before had half its roof blown away. Bill and I stood and gazed at it. Things had happened and were happening so very quickly that nothing surprised us now. Many of our fellows made an appearance from out of the cellar.

"Plenty of booze in the cellar, mates," they shouted.

We were soon in there and armed with three quart bottles of champagne. I forced one in each side pocket and opened the third. This was the first time I had tasted champagne. We stood there, our clothes muddy and dripping. I swilled the drink down. Having had no food or drink for nearly thirty-six hours one would have thought it would have made us drunk. However, strange to relate it did not, although we bolted the best part of half a gallon between us. It made us a little merry but we were soon on the move again.

Half a mile on we were to have another blow for we heard a terrific explosion. What was that? Were the Germans behind us as well as on three sides? No. It could not be that. We looked at each other in dismay, then the awful truth burst on to us.

We now knew that the bridge over the canal had been blown up by our own Royal Engineers to hinder the enemy's advance. This proved to be so, for when we came up to the Canal the big bridge had gone and the canal in flood. What could we do?

Clothes and equipment also lay everywhere here which only too plainly told us if we wanted to go on there was only one way and that was to swim it.

Some badly wounded chaps lay on stretchers. They had been carried as far as possible. They needed help but they had to be left.

We were the extra stragglers of the retreat. Perhaps we had been sacrificed on purpose to try and hold the enemy if only for a few hours. I don't suppose we were expected to be alive by this time if the truth was known.

Lower down several men could be seen swimming through the dark cold water. Many were drowned while attempting to swim this canal. We must soon think about it. Bill was cursing. Just then a violent burst of machine gun fire broke out not many hundred yards away from us. The Germans were in the village we had just left. That decided us who wanted to stop to be taken prisoner or killed. Let them stop who liked – we were going through the water.

I slung my rifle on my back, discarded my gas mask, put my wallet in a waterproof ammunition case and walked into the water, Bill following me. We were soon in deep water, the current very strong. Thank goodness we could both swim well. My clothes hung like lead the two bottles of champagne did not improve matters. Once again I was almost giving up when my feet touched the bottom and we waded out.

CHAPTER VI

OUR RETREAT CONTINUES

WHAT a pickle to be in! Not a dry thread on us. I was cold and my teeth were chattering. "How about a drink, Bill," I said. He did not want one. He mumbled something about a 'gammy' knee. Well we kept on and came to a road leading to God knows where. We never knew and never cared, only we knew others were going that way so I took it that we were right.

The German shell fire had ceased, but his machine gun fire was still to be heard in the village we had just left. Many dead were lying about here, no doubt killed early in the afternoon by shell fire. Dry clothes we wanted and dry clothes we must have at all costs. We must rob the dead to help the living. The first one I approached. No! I couldn't. He was knocked about too badly. Too much blood. We eventually each got a dry tunic and cardigan and took our shirts off and put a cardigan and tunic on. We also helped ourselves to ammunition and a gas mask. Poor fellows, they would never need them again. We turned one over to cover him up with our wet tunics when a portion of a loaf showed from his pack. We were starving. Who could blame us? We took the bread and devoured it in a few minutes. How good it seemed! Bread had never tasted so palatable. It was no good messing about – we had already wasted enough time. It would soon be dark. What should we do then?

"Don't worry, Bill, let's keep on," I said.

Darkness was now almost upon us. Soon we came to a group of soldiers who represented several battalions discussing the best way to proceed. We were absolutely lost.

Still the stragglers kept coming up, and what tales of misery and misfortune each had to tell! Just before six o'clock several chaps came along who had just come through the canal. They informed us that many of their comrades were drowned trying to cross it. They could not bring their Lewis Guns with them. They were obliged to throw them in the water.

It was now dark. How strange the absolute silence was! Everything in this light seemed weird. I think we were all a little 'windy.' Guards were placed lower down the road to prevent a surprise, and twelve of us, Bill and myself included, with an officer, set out to try and find some information as to where we were on the main road. If only the British guns would open out all would be well for us. We could then walk towards the flare of the guns, but our guns were strangely silent.

After a long walk we found the main road. We then commenced our journey back to our comrades and arrived safely. How glad they all were to see us and to know we had found a way to get back. We now lost no time in striking off to get to that road.

We tapped another bottle of champagne, walking along in the slush. Nothing but mud and water. It had now begun to rain. It must have been 10 o'clock by the time we got on that road.

Another half an hour's tramp brought us up to the main body of the troops, all lying on the road resting. What a day everyone of these soldiers had been through! What did to-morrow hold in store for us? Perhaps as bad as to-day. What they were all waiting here for no one seemed to know. Word came round about 12.30 that rations would soon be up. I cannot remember the last meal I had as I lay on the muddy road and wondered where all this would lead us to. Time went on and no signs of rations coming. Oh, how cold and wet I was! I couldn't keep a limb still. If this lot didn't kill us I did not know what would.

I looked at Bill and said, "Open one of your bottles."

"Good that's a little better."

"How long do you think that grub will be?"

It was getting colder and the drizzle of rain made matters worse. I dozed into a kind of sleep, utterly beat. I could feel the damp striking through my clothes but I was too cold and stiff to move. Cold, wet and hungry, but it was a relief to be at rest and those blasted machine guns quiet.

I was almost asleep when I was awakened by horses galloping towards me. Several limbers drawn by two horses were soon amongst us. The rations at last! Thank God. I hoped there was plenty for each man. They might have brought them up before. We wondered why there was not much excitement higher up where the limbers had stopped. I soon knew the reason.

Yes, we could have plenty of rations, yes, as many as we could carry for those rations were Rifle Ammunition and Lewis Guns. Next I heard someone shout, "Come on you men, there. Stick a few bandoleers over your shoulders. You're bound to want them."

Someone wanted to know something about rations.

"I know nothing about food. Think yourself damn lucky you have plenty of ammunition," was the reply.

I dropped down again against Bill.

"Blast 'em," said Bill.

"Any left in that bottle Bill?"

"Yes, just a drop   No, somebody knocked it off. Open one of yours." After that we lay dozing and drinking until daybreak.

"Anybody got any fags?" I asked. I would have given anything for a smoke.

However I was soon supplied with a cigarette and I had no sooner started to smoke when an officer detailed several hundred of us and we were told to follow him.

"Has everyone got plenty of ammunition?" the officer yelled to someone higher up.

"I must have a Lewis Gun or two."

"Sorry," someone answered. "We only had four sent up and they have gone with Jim and Brown." These two were Officers who had taken several hundreds of soldiers to spread a thin line across the Country to try and stop 'Jerry' as he advanced to-day. One might as well have had a bucket and been told to empty the Thames.

We tramped across field after field until we arrived at a single track Railway line. The rails were banked up about five feet with a dyke at each side and a few willow trees. We soon found out we were to hold these lines to-day and not to give them up without a struggle. Terrible fighting had taken place on these lines yesterday. Death arrayed in all its hideous forms met my gaze. The sight was enough to convince one of the horrors of War. Our dead lay all along the line, in fact everywhere. Machine guns had done the damage. As I walked along and saw body after body I could not help but notice they were all the same stamp of youngster; really only boys, but what a resistance these English lads must have put up. That Bulldog spirit which is born in every home from the highest to the lowest in our land had made itself manifest that day.

Eventually rations came up. One small loaf to four with a little jam. What a feed to last a day! It took me about two minutes to 'lose' mine.

Plenty of shovels lay about and we began to dig ourselves in, by the side of the Railway line. The dyke at the bottom was full of the usual 'beverage' – water, therefore the necessity of digging in higher in the bank. Eight of us, including Bill and myself, were detailed off with a Lance-Corporal to go in front, into the Country to see if we could locate where 'Jerry' was.

I looked at Bill, Bill looked at me.

"Another b----- good job," he said.

The Corporal gave us to understand that he was not going far out.

"We will go as far as that farmhouse standing about a quarter of a mile away," he said.

We were to walk, say about twenty yards apart and close round the farm. The Corporal thought this would he the better way. Of course if we met anything before we got to the farm we were to get back as quickly as we could. Yes, very cheerful. There was no doubt it had got to be done so we started. We passed through two fields and nothing happened. The third field was ploughed, lately seeded and rolled. Its fine soil was crushed as fine as a billiard board. British dead lay all over this small field. How had they all come to get killed there and none in the two fields through which we had just come? If yesterday could only speak! The vicinity of these Railway lines was Hell. We were now approaching the farm. We decided to approach it on all sides.

Although smoke was coming from the chimney we knew no one was living in that house. Perhaps the Farm was full of German Soldiers who had even now got us well covered with one or more machine guns?

A pair of horses harnessed to a farm wagon loaded with furniture and bedding stood at the back door. We crowded through the door which led into the kitchen. Inside were two women and a man just ready for flight. The man tried to push by us as if in a dreadful hurry all at once.

The Lance-Corporal decided to question him. He asked them in broken French if they had seen any Germans. They understood us perfectly and said, "Halliman gone miles away."

To us this did not seem quite right. The Corporal was not satisfied.

"Seen any Germans to-day?" he again queried.

"No", they said.

We asked ourselves if they should be allowed to go. They seemed frightened at us British. Why? We could not understand it.

The Corporal turned on the two frightened women ordering them to make coffee for us. The kettle stood on a nice bright fire already boiling. In a few minutes several cups were full of coffee and not having enough cups they supplied jugs. Could they go now we wondered? Why had they stayed so long in their home (if it was their home) when all that desperate fighting had been taking place yesterday? By their own statements to us the Germans were miles away. Things did not seem quite right.

The Corporal said, "I suppose they had better go. I think they are French."

We stood on one side and they did not want telling twice. As they were getting in their conveyance a machine gun barked out not a great way off. It was a German gun. They then struck their horses up and were away but instead of turning the way we expected them to do they went direct towards the German lines. We shouted, "Come back, come back." I know they heard us.

"That's damned funny," I said to myself. We did however find out later they were Germans but unfortunately we did not discover this until it was too late. They were German spies.

"Let's drink our coffee and get back," the Corporal said. "I don't like the look of things," he continued. "Two of you stay outside and keep a sharp look-out," he ordered.

As we entered the Kitchen again we heard a groan coming from the adjoining room.

"Good God, what the hell's that?" I said. The place was getting on everyone's nerves. Several of us slowly made for that room from which the moans still came. We all had our rifles ready. I do not know what we expected but we were all overstrung.

The room was on the small side and a large bed filled nearly half of it. In bed we found a wounded man stripped to the waist looking ill and white. He was shot in the left arm. We crowded round the nearest side of the bed.

"You Halliman?" said the Corporal.

"No, no," he cried. "No Halliman me – me Froggy."

"Why have these folks left you, then?" we asked him. He did not appear to understand. All he kept saying, "Me no Halliman. Me Froggy."

"Well, we will take him back with us, I don't like the look of things here," says the Corporal.

"Go round the other side of the bed Bill and you Fred and help get him out of bed."

As we pulled the bed farther away from the wall, there lay on the floor the field dress uniform of a German Officer of the Bavarian Regiment. His face went all colours. No one spoke. We could hear that machine gun again. If we don't soon move we shall be trapped.

"Pull him out Bill," the Corporal said.

He began to resist and before we knew where we were a revolver came from under the clothes with his right hand and a shot whizzed past us and lodged in the wall, but before any further damage could be done the Corporal shot him through the brain and with that he said, "Come on let's get out, the place seems like hell."

The place seemed to frighten me. I did not like the whole business. I did not like first the unsatisfactory way in which the 'French' people answered us and secondly the direction in which they went and now came all this. It was enough to send a man mad.

We were soon in the yard. That German machine gun was again firing out its metal of destruction. We could plainly make out it was being fired from the dyke in the corner of the next field. We dodged through the farmyard and started back. We hoped to have kept the farmhouse and that damn gun in line until we could get back to our chaps. As we hurried through that small field where so many British lay dead I am sorry to say that I felt real glad we had killed that German Officer. It was just a little bit of our own back. Could such sacrifices go in vain and not be avenged? No. I declared to myself there and then that I would kill all Germans, the dogs. Next minute my thoughts were elsewhere. That gun had sighted us. We scrambled through the hedge – we had still two fields to go through. We kept close to the hedge going along on our hands and knees. That gun meant having us if possible. Thank goodness the ground here was very low, which greatly helped us.

We all got safely through this field but the fire from the machine gun kept following us as we crawled along. One more field still to get across and only a shallow dyke to get in. We each crawled through the hedge and started slowly to get back to the railway line. Rattle, rattle, rattle, that gun sent its bullets all round us. Some one had got hit in the shoulder. I dare not look up to see who it was. We got to the other side of the field at last without anyone else getting hit. Now, the biggest job was to get over the railway line to the other side. We have got to get over somehow. "Blast the gun. Why the hell don't he leave off?" I said to myself. We still lay there discussing one way and another when the gun stopped. Ten minutes or more passed and not a sound. He has given us up we all thought.

"Now's our chance," said the Corporal. "Are we going over those b----- lines or are we going to stop here all day?" he continued.

"Alright then, when I say 'right' we all jump up and get over."

"Right," we jumped to our feet and made a dash over the rails, but as quick as we were, that gun got two of us. The Corporal and another of our party. The Corporal was hit almost as he mounted the bank, but the other fellow nearly got over. We crept up to the top of the bank and pulled him down with us but it was just a case of one more. The Corporal, we had to leave on the other side. We had been out and lost two good men.

Nobody wanted to know what information we found out. Perhaps that Officer who sent us out, knew all he wanted to. Perhaps that machine gun which was firing told him all he required.

So the day went on, but for occasional bursts of machine gun fire and a few German Airplanes coming over, things were quiet. It was getting dusk and we were getting fidgety. We were allaying the German

Advance. Why didn't they put in an appearance before now? Not a mere handful of British troops on the railway line could stop him. Surely he outnumbered us vastly? His dense hoards of troops could have trodden us in the ground by sheer weight of numbers without firing a shot if he had only come on. The British at this moment were practically routed on this sector. Why the Germans did not come on and keep coming on is one of the biggest mistakes he ever made. The German army threw 106 divisions of men in the field at this sector and broke the British back completely. They never realized it. If he had only pushed forward he could have gone to hell. What could such a handful of men hope to do against such unfair odds. No wonder Lord Haig said in a part of his famous message to the British Public at home, "We are in the darkest hours. Many amongst us are now tired. To those I say, 'Victory will belong to the side which holds out the longest!' There is no other course open to us only to fight it out. Every position must be held until the last man, with our backs to the wall and believing in the justice of our cause each one of us must fight on to the end. The safety of our homes and the freedom of mankind depend alike upon the conduct of each one of us at this critical moment."

Darkness came on. A message came up the line from someone. We had got to stick it all night – everyone had got to stand to. Someone had just crept over the lines to have a look at the Corporal. It was what we expected – he was dead.

We were all a little 'windy' I think. The night was very black. The uncertainty of the position was killing – it was not healthy to have 'Jerry' so quiet. The dead which lay about were getting on my nerves. It was my first night amongst the dead. How weird they all looked as the Verey lights from the German lines lit the country up with their ghostly light. My eyes seemed rivetted on them. This night which seemed an eternity to me, at last came to an end. Never had I welcomed daylight so much. How strange everything looked last night! – but it was a case of being a bit 'windy.' How tired we all were – my eyes were very heavy for want of sleep and my lips were cracking for the want of drink. Perhaps rations would come up and water might even come with them. But no luck.

Rations did come up about eight o'clock, but no water. Thirst must be quenched, beggars can't be chosers; dead or no dead laying in it, we must have drink. I went a little lower and had a good drink of that muddy water. Oh! It tasted rotten. We began to look in a pickle our clothes were soaked in mud – buttons on our tunics had gone black and we had several days growth of beard on us. We began to look more like Russian soldiers than the smart trained soldier of the British Army. Bill, who was naturally dark, looked very bad; myself, being on the fair side, did not look quite so bad.

Towards dinner time machine guns began to sweep the Railway lines and a few shells began to drop.

"I expect we are in for it to-day," I said. We had too quiet a day yesterday.

"Look up," a 'Jerry' plane was coming over. He was machine gunning us as well, the swine. Where were all our airmen these days to let the enemy have it all their own way like this?

I could plainly see what was coming off – a repetition of two days ago.

"Look, Bill, look at the sods coming down that hedge there," I said. Our Lewis Guns were firing on them, making them take cover. Hundreds of rifles begin to crack.. 'Jerry' wasn't going to have those lines without having to pay dear for them. Germans were to be seen everywhere – thousands of them, the old square heads, how we hated them. Take that, and that, as I aimed at them in the distance. It was a little too far out to see what damage had been done. So the time went on and the Germans were slowly but surely closing in on us. "Here is that blasted airplane again," I said to myself. He came straight over our lines firing his gun as he swept along. Our rifles blazed away at him. Oh! How I should have liked to have seen him brought down!

"Here he is again and he'll come once too often," I thought to myself. This time he came extra low. Hurray! Our Lewis Guns were pasting him. Thousands of bullets were fired at him.

"He's off Bill. No. Look, he is in trouble. Good lord, he's caught fire."

With that he came down between us and the German lines. It crashed and was a total wreck. The Germans who were once in that plane are now good Germans!

This seemed to madden the Germans, for their shells came much quicker and I am sorry to say many were finding their mark.

By this time many Germans could be seen coming down the same hedge we went down yesterday.

Our rifle fire was being kept up well but it was impossible to take a good aim now, as a score of machine guns were sweeping the top of those Railway lines, thousands of bullets skimming them every minute.

"Bill," I said, "we're done this time."

"Yes, blast 'em. Look at the sods coming down there," he replied. The enemy came nearer and nearer, closing in on us. Our situation grew grave and the more we had to expose ourselves, the greater our losses. We were losing men fast now.

"I am sick of it all now, I wish a bullet would hit me," I said to myself.

It was now somewhere about dinner time and things looked bad. We must have lost quite half our men by now.

The wounded went or were taken farther up the Railway lines. I don't think the stretcher cases could be got away. Shells were being fired point blank from the field guns.

By this time a few Germans had reached the other side of the line and commenced to throw their hand bombs over, causing loss of life and panic. The situation was desperate – the machine gun fire was madder than ever. Every minute I expected him to come charging over the top of those lines.

Someone said, "Fix your bayonets." I fixed mine. Bill fixed his. A lot of good we should be now in a hand to hand fight in our weary condition against fresh troops. I happened to glance to the right at that moment. What few troops of ours were still alive were retreating fast along the railway bank. A hand bomb came over and exploded about thirty yards on our left. Like a flash Bill and I started to run down the bottom of the bank after the other chaps, others of course, following. Every few yards we had to step over our dead who were all hit in the head. Every moment I expected the Germans to sweep over the lines and put 'paid' to us. In a few minutes perhaps their machine gun fire would stop; then they would soon be at us. Good God, the quicker the better. We shall be out of our misery then. Weary and tired, I didn't care what happened.

We had now travelled several hundred yards and a dyke ran away from the Railway lines and our chaps were running down this as fast as the water which was in it would allow. I could see a wood beyond this dyke. If we could only gain that we might get away. My hopes began to rise. Fresh strength seemed to come to me. As long as those guns were sweeping over the Railway lines we were getting away; that's all I cared at the moment. Another five minutes and we should perhaps be clear.

We had now gained the wood and I scrambled through some barbed wire. I caught one of my puttees on the wire and left half of it behind. The other half came undone and fell off as I ran through the wood. How miserable and wet we all were !

Still the shell fire was going on. The Germans no doubt thought we were still defending that Railway. Perhaps they intended taking their time to crush us. Little did they dream that the only defenders on this side of the line were our dead.

We got safely through the wood and carried on down a hedge. Bill was lagging behind, nearly done up.

"Can't go much farther," he said. "I can hardly bend my knee." Slushing through water and mud didn't seem to agree with Bill's rheumatics.

After swearing at him a time or two, I got him along a little faster.

A small farmhouse stood just in front of us. We made for it. We decided to just look in to see if any food could be found. Alas! Our hopes were dashed. We were evidently not first this time. We peeped down the cellar. No cases of champagne met our gaze this time. Nothing, only empty cases and disorder. We were just off when I noticed a stew pot on the grate. I looked in and found a little stew which looked as though it had been there several days. It smelled alright so we decided to take the pot with us. We ate the meat as we went along, only stopping to have a drink out of the pot. This was the first French stew I had. It was 'tres bon,' even if it was a day or two old. We wished there had been twice as much.

"There you are. You see much and want more," I said to myself as Bill remarked that there was not sufficient to satisfy him.

A little farther on we sighted the main road and in a few more minutes we had reached it.

It was one long straight road as far as the eye could see with the British Army on approximately a forty mile front in a complete rout: Staffs Regiment, Duke of Wellington, King's Royal Rifles, Suffolks, Northants. All these were there and many more besides. Staff Officers on horse-back and also Generals. All were there, so complete was this retreat. We were so thick it was like coming out of a Football Ground on a Saturday afternoon. Limbers were hurrying back, saving just what few things they could get away with. Artillery men with the eighteen pounders up to God knows what. There were ambulance motors loaded with wounded unable to move any faster than the others. A dozen nationalities could be noticed in as many yards. I even noticed a few Chinamen – the lousey Devils! How they stank! What a congestion – all with one idea – to get away – every man now for himself. Wounded men lay on the side of the road in scores, many crying out for someone to help them along, and I am sorry to say those who could not walk were left behind for 'Jerry' to take care of.

The situation was desperate – darkness was creeping on us.

Perhaps it was all for the best. The machine gun fire had left off some time now, but a few heavy shells were still coming over. Of course they knew we were on that road. What in the hell would happen if one of these times he followed us up? He would have the whole lot of us, and the War might be finished then. Bill said he hoped they would – he had had enough.

"B----- them," he said. "To Hell with the whole German Army. I am going no farther." With that he fell out and threw himself down on the side of the road.

I tried to persuade him to move and cursed and swore at him. No, he was not going any farther, he said. I tried to pull him up. Bill did not intend to move. Time was creeping on and we were now in the rear of the retreat. The troops were not now so thick. Many refugees were still coming along bringing with them a few personal belongings which they were able to save, so rapid had been the German advance.

I continued to plead to Bill to come along but he was determined to stay where he was. He said he could not go any farther. I threatened to leave him! But it was of no avail.

"Might as well be dead as alive," he said. "Shoot me out of the way."

"He's ill or mad," I thought to myself – and if we did not soon move we should be taken prisoners. Whatever happened I did not intend to leave Bill.

Time went on and troops continued to pass by. I continually kept pleading and arguing with him, but all to the same purpose. Soon we should be alone on that road with the exception of the wounded, and those who had died of wounds.

"What the Hell's up with you Bill, come on think of me." Bill moved. "He's coming," I thought. No, he's sitting down again.

"If you don't come Bill," I said, "I'll shoot you," as I raised my rifle to the level of his head.

"Now or never – your last chance – will you come?"

"No!" he said. "Shoot me and save yourself."

I was in despair – nothing I could say or do, didn't seem to make any impression on him. What could I do?

Darkness was creeping on us – nothing to be heard but the cries of the wounded and the wind howling through the trees.

Once more I turned to him.

"Bill, think of your misses. Don't throw your life away," I continued. "Bill, think of your little girl."

He straightened himself up and it seemed as if something inside him had moved.

"Yes, bless her," he said. "I had forgotten her. To Hell with the Germans! I won't give in. God, my head! Move on, then – slowly."

I pulled him up – his rifle fell off his shoulder and I picked it up and slung it over mine. I put my arm around him and the two of us moved off. Bill could only walk slowly. I think we must have been absolutely the last ones.

It was now quite dusk and but for a groan or two from some wounded men left behind not a sound could be heard. How uncanny!

I did not suppose the Germans would come too far to-night. A little way on I could see a light – it was a fire on the side of the road. What was it for? It was a little too far off in this light to make out what it was. As we approached we found a small fire under a copper. It stood outside a Y.M.C.A. "All are Welcome" I could see written in large white letters on the side of the building. What memories rushed through my brain as I read these words over and over again.

The copper was nearly full of boiling cocoa, sugarless but hot. We soon got two mugs and were drinking mug after mugful. Those Y.M.C.A. People who had stayed practically right to the last and made cocoa for thousands of our boys are worth the V.C.

Bill got a box and drew up against the fire. The warmth was really very comforting. I did not know when last I felt the heat of a fire.

Troubles for the moment were forgotten. 'Jerry' might go to Hell for all we cared. It was now dark.

God, what was that? Something was touching my leg. It was only a large tabby cat. How it made me jump!

"We must be on the move, Bill," I said. He did not answer me. I thought he was going to have another spasm but he slowly rose and we continued up that long road.

We were lost. Yes, lost in France. We had not the slightest idea where we were going and incredible as it seemed we had lost the British Army. That was all. Bill said he did not care a b----- if we never found it again – he had had a belly full. He would be a conscientious objector next time, if ever there was another War!

CHAPTER VII

LOST IN FRANCE

SO we dragged along this seemingly endless road mile after mile. A gun boomed somewhere from the British lines, or better, let us say, British Territory. This was the first British gun I had heard for the last three days. God, those three days seem like three years.

We eventually came to a village. Not a soul was to be seen – the village was ours to do with as we liked. I was about done up and we decided to stay the night somewhere in one of what appeared to be the last few houses left standing – and see what morning brought forth.

We had lost all idea of time. It might have been twelve, two or four for all we knew. It would not have been so bad if we had got a few fags.

We went into a farmhouse not having any matches or lights. One place to us was as good as another. We lay on the floor and in a few moments Bill was snoring. I was nearly asleep when I heard steps coming. I was sure. I wasn't mistaken. Surely 'Jerry' wasn't outside. He must be miles back. For a minute I was as one turned to stone – little cold shivers ran down my back. I wished we hadn't stopped. I grabbed hold of my rifle, released the safety catch and stood just inside the door. Those footsteps were coming closer. Who was it? Friend or foe? I dare not wake Bill up. Whoever it was would soon be on us. As the footsteps grew nearer I could feel my heart beating fast. It was a solitary figure but it was too dark to make out who it was. I decided in a flash to let him come on and then challenge him. I raised my rifle when he was about ten or fifteen yards from me.

"Halt!" I roared out. "Who are you?" He stopped instantly.

"Duke of Wellington," came the reply.

"Come on slowly," I said, not wishing to be caught napping.

"B----- fool you. Can't you believe me?" I knew then everything was alright and he was British. I could see that he had a bandage on his head.

"Where are we?" he said.

"Don't know," I answered.

"Where are the other chaps?"

"On farther, I expect. We're stopping till morning and then going on."

"Come on in. What do you say you belong to?"

"Duke of Wellingtons."

Bill still slept on. He was snoring louder than ever

"No," he said, "not wounded bad. Just a nasty cut on the temple. I found myself down that blasted road. I don't know how long I had been there, but I know I have walked a hell of a long way.

"Have a fag," he said.

The snoring stopped. Thank God for a smoke. Bill was sitting up. The word 'fag' he heard in his sleep.

We were each soon smoking a cigarette. Strange to say all my sleepy feeling had left me. We sat in silence smoking. How good a smoke was when you had not had one for a few days.

A few shells kept going over us but they were dropping a long way off, and we fell off into a doze again.

"Have another fag, mate!"

"Yes, I think we had better."

Dawn began to break and some fowls somewhere in the rear of

the house began to crow.

"Here, Bill, when it's light we had better have a look round."

In another half an hour it was daylight. We soon found that we had paused the night in a decent farmhouse. The furniture was certainly in disorder but I had great hopes of finding some food.

After a thorough search by the three of us no food of any description was found. I suppose we were second again. All we found was some sour beer and ground coffee.

We went a little farther down the road and searched another cottage but we met with very little success. All we found was some stale bread. Well, that was better than nothing, I thought to myself. We eventually decided to go back to the farm and look up those fowls which we heard a short time ago. We found a few old hens and a couple of skinny cockerels walking about at the back of the house. The thing was to catch them for they were as wild as could be. We threw a little of the bread to them to try and coax them to come near us but they did not intend coming too near. However, we could not waste too much time on such trivial matters. I loaded my rifle and handed it over to Bill to do the necessary. Bill took aim and hit the first cockerel in the neck. With that the others flew over the hedge with Bill in pursuit. He fired a second time. This time he blew a hole right through an old hen.

We had to have a fire and for this purpose we broke up a chair to get it started. There was plenty of coal outside.

Jock and I commenced to pluck the fowls. I never thought a fowl had so many feathers!

"Here Bill, come and pull some of these wing feathers out. I bet this old devil was here before the War started."

Feathers were all over the room.

"I can't say this old hen which I am trying to pick looks very appetising." Bill had blown half her chest away. But we were all hungry and not very particular. Bill by this time had a good fire going. I went outside to see how much smoke we were making. We were making plenty but we should have to risk that. I also had a look down the road to see if I could see anyone, but not a soul was about and all was quiet. I went back to Bill and Jock.

"Do you think it's safe to stop an hour or two, Bill?"

"Let's take the blasted fowls on with us."

"Got the wind up?"

"B----- 'Jerry.' We're going to have a feed first, my lad," he said as he held the old hen against the fire bars singeing the feathers off. He treated the other one likewise.

Bill chopped the legs off with his bayonet and went into the yard to a pump to clean them. We got the large saucepan half full of water and waited for Bill. He came back in a few minutes with the carcasses of the fowls –looking much better for a wash. In another minute they were in the pot.

We made the fire up and lodged a little kettle against the pot. Jock started to break up another chair; he preferred wood to coal.

"It won't make so much smoke," he said.

I had another look outside also down the road, but not a soul was in sight. We were as right as rain. I did not expect 'Jerry' would be up here until late in the afternoon and it was now early morning. We went back to the fire and put on some more wood – the kettle started to boil. We made a large jugfull of coffee but could find no sugar and of course no milk. Well it's better than nothing. It's hot and wet and that was more than we had been having the last few days. Jock found us another 'fag' each. Soon we began to smell the fowls. I saw visions of a boiled fowl; not too bad to a man who is nearly starving. How nice the warmth of the fire felt. Something began to itch in my shirt. I must not get too hot for comfort's sake – let them rest!

I decided to have a swill. I found some soap and something which acted as a towel and went to the pump, Bill following suit. The water freshened us up a little – it was the first wash for several days.

"When did you have a shave last, Bill?" I asked him.

"Shut up – can't worry my head about those things," he replied. We put our gas masks back on us as it was never safe to be without one of these handy.

When we arrived back in the room Jock had got plates, knives and forks and set the table for the coming feed. The smell from those fowls seemed better than ever. My insides were fair on the work.

"See if they are done, Bill," I said.

"Course they're not, they're not half done yet," he answered.

Bill lifts the lid tip and sticks a fork in the old hen and holds it out of the water.

"Course she ain't done yet, the old sod is as tough as hell – give them plenty of time," he said.

"That's right," chimed in Jock.

He began to break up a bit more furniture again for the fire. If we had had to stop there long Jock would have broken up all the furniture in the house. The fire was like a furnace and the lid was bumping up and down on the pot.

"I hope they will soon be done now," I said. I was getting a bit fidgety. We had been here plenty long enough.

Jock poured some more coffee out and I went outside again to have a look out for possible danger. I stood in the doorway for about a quarter of an hour and with the exception of a few shells going over all was quiet. "It will be another nice day," I thought to myself as I stood there. I went back into the room again. Jock was still heaping furniture on the fire and Bill was half asleep. All the Germans in the world did not seem to worry those two.

"Do you think they are done now," I asked.

"Shut up – put yer sock in it. Have a drop more coffee and shut yer mouth up," came the reply. I could plainly see it was no use saying anything. I expected they must have it their own way, so I sat down on one of the bedroom chairs which Jock had brought down.

"That's right – make yourself at home," he said, "like Bill. Look at the good boy, he's nearly asleep. 'Jerry' doesn't worry him half as much as he does you."

I sat in the chair a few minutes. I could not rest. It was no use stopping here too long. I got up again and went to have another look down the road. The road was clear with still no one in sight. I think I was a little 'windy,' but I had that feeling that all was not well. When you are done and said all, we were in 'no man's land' with no idea how long Jerry will be before he came along with his blasted machine guns, and the worst part of all we had not the slightest idea of how far the British Army had gone back. Nice thing this. What mugs we must be; fancy losing our fellows. You must be damn sure we are not 'all there,' so my thoughts ran as I stood there.

I went in again. Surely those damned hens would be done by now. I livened Bill and Jock up. The silly b-----, they must be mad. I got in again. All the talking in the world did not make any difference. Bill even wanted me to massage his knee.

"Keep your puttees on you silly blighter and get those old hens out of the pot," I said. I was wild.

Bill mumbled something about being 'windy' and says, "Well we'll have one out, just to please him," he said to Jock. "But they ain't half done."

I trembled to think how long we should have to stop if they were not half done. I could plainly see that whatever happened they had made up their wind, to stay and have a feed. I could not very well go on without them, but I expected in the end we should be taken prisoners.

Out comes the first hen – Bill got hold of the knife and to my horror it did not make any difference on it. It was as hard as hell.

"There you are –won't be ruled. Any silly b----- would know they would not be done yet. In it goes," mutters Bill.

He put it in the pot again and Jock commenced to break up another chair.

Again I went into the doorway and stood there another half an hour. I thought to myself that the time must be getting on and that it must be nearly nine o'clock. Perhaps it might even be ten or later than that.

Jock and Bill hadn't been out for the last hour and a half. Neither of them cared a damn.

I went back into the house once more. The grate was red hot. Bill was sound asleep.

"Well of all the fools," I said to myself. I sat down. I had already said enough.

Jock thinks they must be done at last and Bill gently wakes up.

"Have a look at them again, Bill," I said.

This time Bill brings his bayonet into use and fetches the hen out on the end of it.

"No it's still tough," he said.

"I know it must be done. That damn old hen must be ten years old. Try the other one," I asked.

Bill got the other one out and found that a little better. "We will eat this one and put the hen back again for a few minutes," he said.

Bill started to hack the cockerel up.

"The knife isn't very sharp perhaps," he said. "Of course a little might be the cockerel's fault," he continued.

I was served up with a leg and a little breast. Jock gets the same and Bill takes what is left. We divided the bread and had another cup of that sour coffee and with that the feed commenced. The fowl did not taste very grand Bill thought. It evidently required a little seasoning. I did not understand these things – all I knew was that it did not taste quite right and I knew it was terribly tough. I dare not complain to Bill or he would have wanted to put it back in the pot again. Jock said it was lovely – that was his opinion. Bill took the carcass in his hands and commenced to eat it in that manner.

It did not take us many minutes to put this one out of sight, and immediately Bill got the other one out of the pot.

While Bill was doing this I got up to have another look outside.

One look and my heart stood still. Just what I had expected. The Germans were in the village. Several of them were just going into that cottage where we had found the bread. No doubt they were souvenir hunting.

I rushed back to the room. "The Germans are outside, Bill."

"You don't mean so. Oh! Blast it – how many are there?" he queried.

"I don't know. I saw several go in that cottage," I answered.

I seized my rifle and fully loaded it, one up the spout and ten in the magazine. Bill had mislaid his rifle –Jock had been breaking the chairs up with it. He soon found it at the back of the grate. Jock had not got a rifle and furthermore he could not remember what he had done with it.

Which way were we to go? Back or front? I did not know, and we stood and looked at each other. None of us knew what to do. I proposed we ran upstairs and looked out of the windows –front and back. We could get a much better view that way. We all rushed upstairs, Bill and I looking carefully out of the front window. Not a soul in sight. Surely my eyes had not deceived me, or had I been dreaming that I saw those 'Jerries' go in that cottage. Jock said there was nothing in sight from the window which he was looking out of.

He joined us in the front room.

"What's to be done," I said.

"I am certain I was not deceived; better wait here a few minutes and watch," I said.

We did not have to wait long when four Germans came out of the cottage together and were making straight for where we were. They were no doubt looking to see what they could find. A fifth German came out of the cottage some little distance behind the other four.

"Don't fire yet, Bill, let them come a little nearer. Wait until they get as far as that bush," I said.

The five 'Jerries' came on at a fair pace. A bit of our own back this time, perhaps.

"Shoot to kill the swines."

Two rifles cracked out, and two bodies crashed to the ground. Two more shots and we got two more of the dogs, but the fifth had disappeared.

"Can you make out where that other got to?" Bill asked.

Jock thought he had got in the nearby ditch. We waited. Well, if he was in there he didn't intend showing himself. I considered it would be best if we cleared off and both Bill and Jock agreed. W e went downstairs and decided to go out of the back door. We hoped that we should be able to get away without that German seeing us and Jock led the way.

He had just passed out of the door when a shot rang out and he collapsed in a heap. The poor chap was shot clean through the heart. We pulled him inside but he was done – he never spoke a word, poor devil, just one more. I thought it looked as if we were caught like rats in a trap. That blasted German could see the back door as well as the front and undoubtedly at this very minute had the house covered. It certainly did look as if we were done. In any case we had got to try and get rid of that 'square head' to have a chance to get away. Neither of us spoke. I could still hear the pot boiling away. Our thoughts at this moment were not on boiled fowl.

"It's no good standing here like this. Something has got to be done," I said.

We peeped out of the window but there was still no sign of him. He was far too cunning to show himself so easily.

The four Germans which we shot all lay motionless, apparently killed outright.

We eventually decided to go upstairs again to have a look out of that window but still we could not see him.

"I am certain that he must be in that ditch, just beyond where the dead Germans lay," I said to Bill.

"He can't be anywhere else, and in any case when he shot Jock he must have shown himself," Bill answered.

"Good Lord, I could have swore I saw a movement," I said. Bill was of the same opinion. Suddenly an idea came to my mind. We had got to make that 'Jerry' show himself.

I explained to Bill what I had in my head and he agreed that it was a good idea.

"Well, in any case it's our only chance," he said.

As long as that German lay outside with the whole house covered, we were doomed. It could not be long now before other German troops came into the village.

My plan was briefly this: I was reckless, and being the better shot of the two I was to go upstairs and cover that ditch with my rifle. Bill was to hold Jock's dead body just outside the back door to try and draw the German's fire. It was no doubt a terrible plan, but it was our only chance. Again the dead must help the living.

Bill put Jock's tin hat on and commenced to move him to the back door. I felt sick – Bill was going to show Jock's head and shoulders just outside the door as a target and it was up to me to see that German sniper didn't have first shot. I was now in the bedroom – I had my rifle on my shoulder – I had even taken the first pressure on the trigger. I did not mean to give that German half a chance if I could help it. He had already done enough damage. Now I had the whole ditch covered – I could hear Bill moving about downstairs – I prayed that things might happen quickly. Minutes were passing which seemed like hours when Bill shouted out, "Look out, careful now Fred."

My nerves seemed at breaking point. I had to be calm. Not only for ourselves but I couldn't allow Jock to be knocked about even if he was dead. Still nothing happened and just as I began to despair I saw something move a little higher up in the ditch – so slight, but I am sure I was not deceived. Yes. There it is again – a little more of it this time – a German tin hat – more and more of it slowly appears. I took careful aim. As soon as his face appears I say to myself, "I will." I pulled the trigger. Crack! God! He's still there. Have I missed?

I take aim again and fire, and still he's there.

Bill came running upstairs – I show him. I could not understand it. I fired two or three times again to make sure. Bill did the same. Still we could make out that tin hat and half a face.

"Strange. Let's get out. Do you think it's safe?" I asked.

"Must be. You're sure he's as dead as mutton."

We had put eight or nine shots into him. I had a peep out of the downstairs window. I could just make out the top of the tin hat. We calmly walked outside with our rifles handy. Still we could see that tin hat. It seemed to fascinate us. Bill meant to have a look. I did not know what to say. We slowly made our way towards the object. We passed those four dead 'Jerries' – I shuddered –our rifles covered that tin hat. We were only a few yards off. The sight I shall never forget. A German lay there holding a rifle – dead – his face looking hideous and covered with blood. A hole as big as a tennis ball was in his forehead where most of our bullets had struck him. Several had gone through his tin hat. No doubt my first shot had hit him between the eyes, killing him instantly – he remained in the exact position as he died.

I could see he had a revolver on him – just what I wanted – it was a beauty of the magazine type. Bill also wanted one and he soon got one off one of the other dead Germans. We also obtained two daggers and a loaf of black bread.

"Come on," I said. "Let's get away."

We moved off. Bill said he was going to fetch the old hen which he had nearly left behind. I was wishing he had forgot it – I was anxious to get away now while we had the chance.

We went in the front way of the farmhouse once more. Bill grabbed hold of the old hen and made his way through the back door, I following him.

I had one look round and there I saw poor Jock lying in a heap in the doorway.

It was no use getting like this. We half walked – half ran down the side of the road.

Thank God we were leaving that farmhouse – the farther away the better. I hurriedly looked behind and we were getting a good way off. I could just see the smoke coming out of the chimney.

"Bill I wonder what the time is now?" I asked.

"No idea – it seems ages since last night."

My mind began to go all over it again. On and on we go farther down the road, the village we had just left now being out of sight.

"Look Bill, there's some of our chaps."

Thank God! Some of our chaps in sight. How comforting it seemed to see them once again.

Bill was now in a better mood and walking well – at the same time examining the 'Jerry' revolver.

"It's a good 'un," he said.

He took the magazine out, but could not put it back. I don't know how many rounds he said there were in it but the whole thing pleased him.

We soon got up to our fellows – they were in all sorts of places. Some had dug holes, others in ditches and dykes, in fact anywhere where there was cover. I could not see any of our Regiment. There were all sorts but none of our mob. I could see Bedfords, Northants, Duke of Wellington, Staffs, King's Royal Rifles and many more as we walked along the line, not quite knowing what to do. The line ran straight off the road to a large farmhouse and buildings. We decided to make our way to it, Bill still carrying the carcass of the old hen under his arm and I the German loaf. We had a word with one another as we walked towards the buildings. We soon learned off one chap that our troops had orders to lie low as 'Jerry' had been seen that morning across the fields about in line, I thought, with the farm we had just left.

"Oh! Blast 'em!" said Bill.

"Who gave those orders?" I asked.

"Only a Second Lieutenant," came the reply.

"Is he in charge here?"

"I don't know. I've been here since yesterday and he's the only one I've seen," came the reply.

"Any chance of getting any rations – that's what we're aiming at?"

"Some hopes. They came up first thing this morning. What there was in it ran out about 5 to a loaf. He's gone that way – try him if you like."

We proceeded on until we got to the farm yard. I handed Bill the loaf. I was going on to see the officer to try our luck when he came round the corner and ran plump into us. I saluted him. Bill tried to and dropped the hen.

"What do you chaps want walking about?" he said.

"Just come in, sir. Any chance of some rations?"

"No. All gone. It doesn't look as though you want any grub" – as Bill picked the hen up – "Where have you been?"

We told him the tale. I do not expect he was a bad chap. He was like everything else – all upside down.

No one knew what to-morrow would bring forth, if to-morrow ever came.

"Ah! well. You had better get inside the buildings and wait until I come back, and don't start looting as soon as you get in either," he said with a twinkle in his eye.

Off he goes and we made our way to the house. Half a dozen chaps were in there sitting down, a Lewis Gun and pans of ammunition standing up the corner. They were drinking beer – they had got a small barrel from somewhere. They handed a jugful over. French Beer is not bad and this went down alright. It was weak but it was wet and had got some sort of a taste. We started to eat the hen. Bill thought it time we did it in. We also ate the German loaf which did not taste too bad either. We gave each of the chaps a little piece to try. More beer came up from the cellar. They told us this cellar was packed with champagne and wine yesterday when they first came in. Of course, all that was a thing of the past now.

"That's about done the hen in. It's been a lot of trouble," said Bill as he handed the remains over to another chap to let him have a go at it.

"I bet he won't find much on her now," he continued.

Two of the chaps who were with us were Duke of Wellingtons. They said they knew Jock Perkins. We described him as well as we could. Yes, of course they knew.

"One of the best," they said. "Used to play centre forward for so-and-so. You don't mean to say he's killed." They could hardly believe it.

"There'll he no b----- left if we keep on much longer," said one of them. I could picture Jock laying in that doorway now.

"Oh! Shut up. Talk about something else," said Bill.

All the live stock on this farm was still here I found out. I went into the farm yard just to have a look round. The pigstyes were full of pigs – all white, and they looked like the Yorkshire breed. There must have been forty or fifty of them – all sizes, from stores up to large breeding sows. There were also six nice calves and as they heard me they rushed to the door. I suppose they expected I had come to feed them. Some real nice poultry walked about and I noticed some half grown cockerels – a big difference to that old hen and cockerel which we boiled in the morning. A large dog was still on his lead and appeared friendly and looked pleased to see me. I let him off the lead. How he raced and danced about. In a little paddock at the rear stood fifteen head of cattle, some half grown, others milking cows. I could see that some of these hadn't been milked to-day. Their bags were full and milk was running away from several. What a shame all these to have to be left behind for 'Jerry.' I expect he would have them in a few hours time. I decided to fetch Bill and let him have a look round. Bill eventually came out with me but the pigs and calves didn't worry him much, but what did concern him was the poultry.

"They're real good. We'll have one or two of those devils before we go back. It's a shame to let 'Jerry' have all of them," he said.

I took him and showed him the cows, and we decided to have a drop of milk later in the clay, when we had got the taste of the beer out of our mouths. No one had any idea of the time but I felt that it would be about the middle of the afternoon. So far 'Jerry' hadn't put in an appearance. Perhaps he might let us rest to-day and come on to-morrow or he might come one of these times at night.

After a time we went back into the house again, where there was still plenty of beer but as it was not good enough we decided to have a lie down for a little while.

I think I must have fallen off to sleep when I heard voices which roused me I looked and saw a Captain in the room with the officer we had asked about rations.

"Is this the Lewis gun team?" I head him say.

Bill and I were only half awake. The Officer pointed to the other fellows and said, "Yes, Sir. Number One. The one with the gun, that's number two there and the others carried the ammunition."

"Yes, very good Clark, that will do now. What about the other gun?"

He turned round and faced us.

"W ho are these two? Just come in you say. This man had better have the other Lewis Gun," he said pointing to Bill.

"Me, sir?" looking aghast. "I have never fired out of a blooming Lewis Gun in my life. Good lord, give it to someone else."

I knew Bill, like all of us, had had one lesson on how to fire the gun – it is a thing we were all supposed to know. If we did not take that gun it's a certainty we should be moved outside and somebody else come in. It would be much better to be inside at night than sit shivering in a cold trench. I meant to take it if he offered it to me. There were ways and means of getting rid of the gun on to someone else – perhaps when the Captain's back was turned. He looked mad and turned to me saying, "Do you think you could manage it?"

"Yes, sir, I think I can. I don't know a great lot about them but I think I know enough to manage them."

"Alright then, you are Number One."

"You," pointing to Bill, "Number Two and two of you others will help with the ammunition. My runner will be up with the gun in about half an hour."

"You will see Clark, these men have their orders."

"Yes, sir," and off he went with Second Lieutenant Clark

following him.

"Well this is a nice b----- pickle to be in," said Bill. "It's bad enough dragging ourselves about let alone carrying a gun – good lor' they weigh nearly a hundredweight.

"Somebody had got to have it. If we hadn't taken it we would have been moved out here. We can pack it on somebody else to-morrow."

The chap with the other gun brought his and put it on the table to show us how to load and fire it.

"Don't learn too much," Bill said, "we don't want to go in no gun team."

Soon our gun came up with two more chaps carrying pans of ammunition, Lieutenant Clark with them. They handed the gun over to me and dropped the ammunition on the floor, no doubt glad to get rid of it, and stood back. They were told they could go back to where they came from. The Officer beckoned us to follow him. I put the gun on my shoulder, also my rifle. I did not mean to lose that. Bill's face was a study as he struggled to put the sixteen pans of ammunition on his back.

"Well, this is a bit of alright," he said.

CHAPTER VIII

A NIGHT AT THE FARM

THE Officer required one gun in the corner of the farm yard and the other one to fire from the end of the pigstye. Our orders were to fire occasional bursts all night into the country in front of us. We were instructed to try and hold out until the following afternoon when a battalion of Guards with Vickers Guns would come up to support us. We were to have the pigstye. There were two large sows in this one and they were making a terrible lot of noise as I expect it was their feeding time. We let them out and soon found a yard brush and shovel and cleaned out the stye. Bill brought a large bundle of clean wheat straw which made us as comfortable as could reasonably be expected. We knocked a few bricks out of the wall-enough to place the gun in. Bill suggested that we should have another bundle of straw and make a good job of it.

We had a fairly good view of the country in front of us. A hedge ran away from us just on our left. Right in front of us were several small belts of trees and bushes. Hedges ran right across our front beyond the belts of trees. This is as far as we thought the Germans had advanced.

Bill had been out for a further look round and when he returned he had a large milk bucket with him.

"Better have a drop of milk. Oh! yes, it's quite alright. There's a quiet old cow. She won't move. I tried her out but she wouldn't let her milk down. I didn't pull them right."

You could trust Bill to have something for nothing if there was half a chance. Our mate who used to work on a farm at home knew all about cows. We followed him to the back of the farm and the cow still stood there where Bill had tried her. Our mate approached her quietly, speaking as he stepped forward. Eventually he had a bucketful of milk which I should say held about three and a half gallons. The cow had not been milked I expect for about a day or two. Bill could not understand how it was our mate had obtained a whole bucketful of milk and he could only get a few drops.

We went back into the house when we learned that some rations were up and we went a little farther down the line where a Sergeant was distributing them. Our pals with the other gun had just got theirs – a loaf and a half of bread for six, in other words four men to a loaf of bread.

"Who is it for?" asked the Sergeant. "Lewis Gun team of six at the farm."

"Alright," he replied

I get my turn.

"Lewis Gun team of four."

"That's not the same lot as just got theirs," said the Sergeant looking rather suspicious.

"No."

"That's alright then.

Bill also stood in the queue in an attempt to get another half loaf. I knew what his idea was. Bill's turn arrives.

"Lewis Gun team of four."

"Where?"

"Farmhouse."

"Another Lewis Gun. How many blasted guns are there up that farm?" roared the Sergeant.

"Well I suppose we've got to live," Bill said.

However, he got his loaf and a piece of margarine alright. He came back all smiles, for Number two gun in the pigstye was in 'clover' as the saying goes. Two to a loaf. Not bad we thought.

We decided that we would not bother the fowls today –we had half a loaf of bread with margarine and some milk.

It was now late in the afternoon and things had been quiet again. One or two German airplanes were flying rather high and a few shells were dropping over.

What a Hell of a noise the pigs and the calves were making! One could hardly hear oneself speak. We let the calves loose and drove them in the paddock at the back. The pigs we did not hardly know what to do with. Anyhow we threw a lot of mangle wurtzel over which quietened them.

The next thing word came up that we had got to stop wandering about as 'Jerry' had been sighted in one of the belts of trees. We were to stand to with the Lewis Guns and as soon as it was dark to send out a few bursts of bullets. We knocked a few more bricks out of the wall so that we could see better. We then put a large bundle of straw in the doorway to stop the draught. We decided then to try the gun once more before it got too dark. We put the pan on alright, released the safety catch and I rested the gun on the wall and aimed it at those trees which stand well out. I pulled the trigger and the gun gave a mad roar and sent out its metal of destruction. I could hardly hold the devil. All of a sudden it stopped.

"What's up now?" I said to Bill.

"Why you fool you've emptied a whole pan. You'll use all the ammunition up we've got in a few minutes at that rate. Press your trigger and release it. Fire the gun in bursts," he replied. Bill told me all this, yet he had led that officer to believe that he knew nothing about it.

We then decided to reload the gun and then have something to eat – we were fairly comfortable in the straw – it was now quite dark and we all began to eat.

The Germans were sending all manner of colour lights up in the sky –they looked quite pretty. I wondered what they were all about. A few very bright lights were being sent up which appeared to come from the belt of trees which stood on our right.

Number One Gun was now firing in bursts, sweeping the country in front of it.

"Yes, that sounds better I think."

Three of us rested while one watched through the gap in the wall. We fired the gun at intervals, and Bill who took a turn, appeared to manipulate it better than any of us. If you could get over Bill, you could get over the Devil.

"That's the way to fire the old sod," he said.

The Officer visited us and wanted to know why the gun was not being fired more but we told him that we had not much ammunition to waste.

"How is that?" he said.

There was silence in the stye for quite half a minute then

Bill said, "We can't get ammunition if there ain't any."

"Who is that speaking like that?" the Officer retorted. No one answered.

"Carry on. Do your best," he said as he went away. "Good riddance, who the Hell does he reckon he is?" said Bill.

Bill was feeling very impatient and he picks the gun up and fires two pans right off the reel. The ammunition would not last another hour at this rate. Those two panfuls were just for luck, Bill argued.

"You know a soldier's farewell, 'Good-bye and b----- you,'" Bill said.

Some one came up from Number One Gun to have a drink out of the milk bucket. The milk was getting short and three and a half gallons had nearly gone, so Bill and our mate decided to go and fetch some more. They came back about an hour later with approximately a gallon.

"Hell of a job in the dark – couldn't find the old cow. The first we got to wouldn't stand still above half a minute and then started to kick. We found one but this is all she would give. We must try again in the morning," Bill narrated.

I had a drink out of the bucket of the lukewarm milk but there were plenty of bits of something in it. But still we could not be too particular.

It would probably be about midnight when 'Jerry' commenced to do a bit of machine gunning. Somebody was coming through the farm yard we could tell before they got to us. The pigs in the first stye always started to grunt when anybody was about. There was no need to challenge them as we could recognise the voices. It transpired that they were two fellows with a few more pans of ammunition. We took eight pans in and sent the remainder to Number One Gun.

All was now quiet with the exception of the grunt of a pig.

Something or someone was pushing their way through the hedge about fifty yards down the hedge which ran away from us on our left. There was no mistaking the noise – someone was there – none of our chaps were out. Was 'Jerry' making a night raid we wondered. The gun was fully loaded and I fancied I made out a movement. I pulled the trigger and one whole pan of ammunition blazed at this particular point. Number One Gun was now firing – they had heard something. Our gun was loaded again and once more that noise. Again we fire our gun, the bullets from it beating the hedge unmercifully. Then came that familiar grunt, grunt. It must have been those two damned old sows which we turned out of their stye this afternoon. Blast them. It cost us two whole pans of ammunition.

Within a minute or two we had that Officer running up to see if anything was the matter and the silly devil gives us orders to go down that hedge a little way to see what it was. Bill and another chap from our gun went with two from number one. They went slowly down the hedge when a grunt greeted them. They found what they expected – the two sows. One was killed outright and the other lay wounded in the bottom of the hedge. The chaps were quickly back again and the Officer went away satisfied.

The night wore on and we were taking it in turns in firing the gun. Dawn would now soon be breaking – the cocks had started crowing – the trees and other objects became more visible. We kept a sharp look out now – the whole lot of us. This was one of 'Jerry's' favourite times to attack. The break of dawn and it has now become quite light. There were no 'Jerries' in sight but I could see the old sow which we had killed in the night lying this side of the hedge. I could not see the other one. Everything seemed suddenly to have come to life. Many birds could be heard singing and those pigs had started grunting again, the calves could be heard piteously asking for someone to feed them. We could shut our ears to the noise of the calves but the blasted row of the pigs squealing and grunting got on our nerves.

That's better, I thought to myself as two fellows from Number One Gun threw plenty of roots over to them. They were soon quiet.

We were all supposed to be standing to, but Bill thought it best if we had another bucket of milk before it got too late, so he and the other fellow went to complete the task of milking that cow once more. They were back in a quarter of an hour this time. Bill said, smilingly, "We found the old cow this time."

Another hour passed by and things were still quiet. Bill thought the old sow looked tempting and said that if we did not have some of it somebody else would take the lot. With this I knew he meant 'Jerry.' We left the gun in charge of the other two fellows. Bill remembered seeing a useful-looking knife in the kitchen. He obtained this and gave it a rub on the doorstep. We soon made our way over to the pig. Bill suggested that a leg would he sufficient so I got hold of it by the hock while he cuts it off with the carving knife. We carried it back with us to the kitchen and with plenty of cooking utensils about we decided to fry some. I found a frying pan with plenty of grease in it.

"It's got to be a little fire this morning – all dry wood which will burn without coal this time," I said to Bill as I lit the fire with a little paper and dry wood which I had chopped up into small pieces. The fire flared and I kept putting small pieces of wood on. I went outside and found there was practically no smoke. Good! I thought to myself. I went back into the house and by this time Bill had got the pan on the fire with plenty of lean pork in it. He had cut the bone in the middle of the leg out and cut off the rind on the outside. We kept the fire flaring brightly and to do this we had to chop up a small piece of furniture. The pork was soon thoroughly cooked when we took it out of the pan and put two pieces of bread in. Bill said he was very fond of fried bread. I could see that we were going to have a substantial meal. We boiled the kettle and later we had a good jug of coffee with plenty of milk. What a feed! – practically under the very eyes of the Germans. Fried bread, pork and hot coffee for breakfast! We took our meal with us across to the pigstye and the eyes nearly bolted out of the heads of the other chaps. "Where did you get that from?" they asked. We told them what we had done and they hastily borrowed the carving knife and fetched the other leg. As they came back I told them to be careful with the fire.

I really enjoyed my breakfast. How it reminded me of old times to have fried bread again. All we wanted now was a few fags just to top it up. I felt a little sleepy but I dare not give way to it. Time quickly passed and I was dozing again when such a hell of a row broke on my ears.

The other two chaps came rushing in with that blasted Officer after them. He had caught them frying their piece of pork and sent them back to their post.

"What do you mean by it – lighting a fire? You will have every b------ German gun on us in no time. Where's your sense? I'll report both of you when you get out of here – and keep out of the blasted house. Now stop here (pointing to Bill and I) with those other fellows and do your duty like they are doing."

He then went to Number One Gun to see what fault he could find there. Bill began to grin and the other two began to swear. If they had done half the things to that Officer they said they would do I think he would have a terrible death.

"What have you done with your pork?" I asked them.

"The damn fool came in the house and kicked the kettle off the stove and picked the pan up and threw the lot on the top of that manure heap, the old sod," was the answer. It was plain to see that the tempers of Number Two Team were not of the best.

Soon we had another visit from him but this time there was a Captain with him. Now for it, I thought. Nothing of the sort however. He was just making his finale inspection of the Gun Teams because he knew that things would soon develop as 'Jerry' had been sighted a little farther down.

"All right in here?"

"Yes, sir."

"Keep the gun going when the Boches show themselves."

"You see we are short of machine guns," I heard the Officer say as they walked away. An hour later more ammunition was sent up to us.

Hullo! Number One Gun is firing. So far as I could make out there were a few Germans in that belt of trees. They soon took cover. Now there were more and we started firing our gun, and then the German machine guns replied. A Lewis Gun commenced firing farther down the line. To me it looked like a general advance and it looked as though the 'fun' was about to start. Shells began to come, the majority falling well over. One dropped within fifty yards of the farm – too near to be pleasant! They commenced to come over even faster. I did not like the look of this. One dropped just in front of Number One Gun. He was getting the range.

"I hope he isn't going to play on the farmhouse. If he does we are in for a warm time," I said to myself. There they come right and left, and two dropped just in front of our pigstye. We ducked low. Earth and shrapnel fell on the roof of the pigstyes. The enemy machine gun fire had also increased, a burst of bullets going through the kitchen window. Eventually a shell struck the farmhouse taking away with it a part of the roof. The shell fire was terrific. A bunch of 'Jerries' were seen making for that long hedge which ran away from us on our left. Our Lewis Gun was trained on them and they scattered. We were using up our ammunition rather quickly, I thought. As long as we could keep the Germans the other side of that belt of trees we were alright. They were trying hard to gain possession of that hedge and they made a further attempt. Both our guns sent their metal of death out. We broke up his advance again and he retired to the trees once more. Many were left behind.

Crash!

A shell hit the house, going in one side and out of the other. It was now a heap of ruins.

There was another shell coming.

Crash!

Right in the middle of the yard. Shrapnel, earth and manure covered the place where we were lying.

"This is getting a bit hot. In any case we've got to keep our gun going," I said.

The Germans attacked again and great masses of troops could now be seen. Both Lewis guns blazed away and they must have taken a great toll of life as our deadly bullets were hurled through space into those great masses of men.

Again he was repulsed.

Thank God the shelling had quietened, but at the same time our ammunition was getting low. I saw a wounded man going back on a stretcher. Those blasted shells were Hell. He had started to shell us again and was dropping shells all round us. The very ground seemed to he churned upside down.

"We shall be lucky if we get out of this lot," I said.

We kept as low as possible except for those brief minutes when there was a lull in the shelling and we fired our gun. Our machine guns had to be kept going at all costs. The shelling was now terrific again and it seemed impossible for anything to live through it.

A shell dropped practically on top of Number One Gun putting everything out of action. Immediately we could hear someone crying out for help, and at that very moment I could see a Red Cross chap trying to reach them. Shells and bullets were flying everywhere but in spite of all this duty called him and he did it without flinching. The air was full of smoke and gas. No doubt the Germans meant attacking again while the barrage was being kept up. They made for that hedge again and our gun rattled out once more, but we only had one gun now –we sadly missed Number One. As much destruction as our gun was doing it was not sufficient to prevent the enemy gaining his objective. The Officer came in with two men carrying a few more pans of ammunition. Whatever happened our gun had to be kept going.

A battalion of Guards were coming up with Vickers Guns to help us out we were told.

All the Lewis Guns lower down the line were holding out – only Number One was put out of action so far – we learnt later that all the team were dead.

We drew the Officer's attention to the Germans who had gained that dyke which ran up the hedge on our left. After a brief stay they left us to do the best we could. We kept the gun going. Time slipped by and in the middle of the afternoon, perhaps, the German shelling quietened. I thought that as long as our ammunition held out we were certain to hold our front in the daylight. The thought that we may have another night here made me shudder, I could not bear to think of it. All of a sudden a mighty noise of machine guns commenced to fire at the rear of us – it started all of a sudden – it was the battalion of Guards with Vickers Guns. What a terrible noise they made. Their bullets swept the country in front of them. Nothing on top of the ground could have lived through such fire. This was kept up without the slightest break until within about an hour of dark, then they left us just as quickly as they came – we were left to deal with the situation as well as was possible. How tame our single gun seemed when they ceased fire.

    I glanced about me and found that our men had once again begun to retire – it was no use stopping on our own so I picked up the gun – the others the ammunition and retired along with them. We had only three pans of ammunition left. We were across the yard into the paddock in no time. Here all the cattle lay dead, many blown to pieces. The house and paddock had received full force of their barrage. We ran across two fields and eventually came to the road again. On all sides was the now familiar sight of troops running back – every man for himself –each were running for their life. I saw some motor lorries going down the road – they contained the Guards with the Vickers Guns. The British Army did not mean to lose them if they could possibly avoid it. So down that road we went –sometimes walking sometimes running. I handed the gun over to one of the other fellows – the weight of it was beginning to tell its tale on me. "Blast the gun," I thought. I intended to get rid of it as soon as a convenient time arose. Shells began to drop all round the vicinity of the road. It was strange how 'Jerry' knew all these roads. "Thank God it will soon be dark again," I said to myself. It would certainly give us a chance to get away. The thought flashed into my mind that I had left my rifle behind but on looking round I saw Bill had it.

    That night we made our bed in a ploughed field. How cold the air was! "I wish I could sleep like Bill," I thought to myself.

    "Oh! damn 'em – here's somebody coming round dishing rifle ammunition. Why the Hell don't they bring some grub up," Bill grumbled. Following the distribution of ammunition was the rum ration which was given out by a Sergeant. I woke Bill up after a short doze and we each had a spoonful. I swallowed mine – the thick firey stuff put new life into us.

    "If they had fed me on that stuff since a baby I should 'ave been a b----- general now," said Bill.

No rations seemed to come up and we again lay down on the wet ground. As dawn broke I was shivering with cold. What a state to be in – hungry, tired and dirty – no overcoat – our clothes wet and thick with mud, myself with only one puttee on – my shirt felt as if it were alive, and there was absolutely no prospect of getting a change. What an outlook.

As time dragged on more and more troops put in an appearance – they had all spent the night somewhere. What a terrible looking lot we were – everyone was splashed from head to foot. It had been four or five days since anyone had a shave.

A little later we were lined up on the roadside and we appeared to be the only Lewis Gun Team about. This made me wonder what had been the fate of the other gun teams which were below us yesterday. I learned later in the day that two of the teams had suffered the same fate as our Number One Gun – blown to pieces. The Officer put us on the extreme right and a few more pans of ammunition were brought to us from somewhere. We were ordered to be careful with it.

"Jerry's coming down by those willows," someone shouted.

"Good Lor', yes," somebody else uttered.

There were twenty or more of them – they were a fair distance off but they kept coming towards us without taking any cover at all.

"Strange!" I thought. "Of all the saucy things."

We trained our gun on them and there we waited to give them a warm reception at the word "fire." The Officer still waited a few more seconds, looking puzzled.

I thought to myself that they were prisoners, coming to give themselves up. We had not enough food for ourselves, let alone feeding prisoners.

"Sight!" he said.

"Fire!"

Bill was firing the gun. He fired the whole pan out in one burst. Many were hit and killed. What few that were left could now be seen waving their arms in the air. We now realized that a great mistake had been made. Those who we thought were Germans were Portugese troops. They wore a uniform which at a distance resembled the field grey of the Germans. Many must have been killed like this. The best thing for us to do under the circumstances was for us to forget it as soon as possible. The remaining few Portugese troops came in but they did not remain behind to help us out – they hurried off, while their wounded were still lying about against those willow trees.

Two staff Officers came up on horseback and we guessed that further developments were expected. It was soon out – a counter attack was to be made. Here were a few hundred of us going to attack. Of all the mad schemes I thought this was one of them but there was of course no alternative for us but to see it through. We also learned that some more of our fellows were attacking him about a mile lower down. Our retreat had gone on from day to day and that the whole British Army was threatened we knew and this was the first time an attempt was being made to turn the tide. A few boxes of Mills hand bombs were given out. Our objective was the road and buildings which lay about half a mile on. We were to try and take that. The Boches could plainly be seen – there must have been thousands of them. The whole business looked hopeless – we were going to attack them under a barrage of Vickers Guns from our rear with a few shells. If we were successful we were to try and hold on – if we were not successful; well, it was good luck to you. The attack, or better, the counter attack was to be made at 11.20. Surely there never was a more strange one. Men of twenty different battalions were in it – practically all were strangers to each other, but all with only one purpose. An Officer was in charge on the extreme right, a Sergeant in the centre and a Corporal on the left. The Officer was continually looking at his watch – a few more minutes perhaps and we should be on our way. The quicker the better for it was nerve-racking. Two minutes yet. No one spoke. How long those minutes seemed to me – they seemed more like two hours. Half a minute now – we shall soon be off.

The Vickers Gunners had opened their maddening fire – they were giving us a good barrage. Men right on our left had run fifty yards forward and were now taking cover. Other sections of the line had rushed forward. It would soon be our turn now. Another section raced forward and were lying down, then another and our turn next.

I held the gun tight waiting for the signal – there it goes up – we all jumped – it reminded me more like a sprint in an obstacle race at school. We all got level with the others and threw ourselves flat on the ground. Our left flank went forward and the Boche commenced to machine gun our frail line – men began to fall but still our advance was maintained. We ran forward again. How heavy that blasted gun seemed to me. Our Vickers Guns were doing wonders and soon we would be half way across that great stretch of country.

Forward, forward, ever forward, that seemed our only thought. We were losing men fast now – large gaps were now in the ranks. Failure! We dare not think of it. We could not go back without our Vickers Guns to support us. It meant only one thing we had got to gain that road and drive the Germans out of it or die in the attempt.

The Sergeant in the middle of our line was dead – that portion of the line being led by a Private of the Suffolks. What wonders these few handfuls of men were performing. By this time we must have been three parts of the way across, perhaps more when the Boche bolted back. How we pasted them. Three whole pans our gun drilled into them – they fell like flies. Our Vickers gave them their final dose of lead, also we were all now advancing. How weary I felt but relieved to think perhaps the worst was over. We had gained our objective –Germans lay everywhere, dead and wounded. A wounded Boche was firing from the dyke just on the other side of the road. The rotten square-head had shot our Officer, so we gave him two or three Mills bombs and that quietened him. There were another party of Germans on our right which we had passed by in our attack. They appeared to be all coming to give themselves up.

"Can't trust the swines. Look at our dead Officer." I said.

"Give it 'em," Bill said.

They were barely forty yards away and our gun blazed out at point blank range dealing death to them. We saw red. Revenge was ours. We were mad. We riddled their hides with bullets. Our gun ceased fire and a German was still standing. Bill threw a Mills bomb and it nearly blew him to pieces. Bill sent over another amongst them, just for luck he told me. Not one remained standing – what a gruesome sight, a sight that will live in my memory for ever. Everyone was there to Kill, Kill, Kill. We hated the enemy, they hated us and each one would kill the other on sight in what they believed to be a just cause.

Huge masses of German troops could now be seen retreating. This was his first reverse since he started his great push. What would happen next, God only knew. We could hardly be expected to hold this position long against the enemy's overwhelming numbers. The British Tommy did not mind four to one but 20 to one is too much, even for him. It was no use worrying. We began to go through the German dead that lay handy in search of souvenirs. Someone a little lower down had obtained a German automatic revolver, similar to the ones Bill and I had obtained previously. All kinds of things were taken off the dead – daggers, watches, money and one fellow even took a gold ring off a finger of one of the enemy. Myself I obtained a solid gold wristlet watch on which was engraved the name of a well-known London firm. As I was taking the watch off him he groans – he was not yet dead and appeared to have bullet wounds in the chest. For all I cared it did not matter to me whether he lived or not but, then, perhaps it would be best if he was out of the way. He no doubt obtained the watch off one of our dead chaps – they nearly all had something which once belonged to a British Tommy.

Bill was more inclined to think about his stomach, and he took a loaf and a tin of grease and with that we sat down and had a snack. What we did not eat we divided and put in our pockets. The majority of the troops were resting and 'Jerry' had gone well back again. Everything was quiet again and comparatively peaceful. What a contrast to an hour or two ago.

It was well into the middle of the afternoon by the watch which I had taken off the 'Jerry' which indicated the time as being 3.30.

Eventually orders came along the line that if nothing happened before dark came we were retiring as the position could not be held. The sooner the better. It could not come too quick for me.

We could hear pigs squealing in the distance and from this we gathered that 'Jerry' was having a feed. We could tell by the noise they were making that the pigs were being killed on a wholesale scale. The pork was obviously for the officers' mess – I believe the Germans were fond of pork. It would soon be dark and everyone was keenly looking out for any possible danger. I crept along a little under cover then I walked in a bending position to where our Officer lay wounded. He was badly wounded and would not get over it but we were determined to try and take him back with us. He was still conscious and wanted to know all that had happened. We tried to cheer him up by telling him that he would soon be home – his wound was of the real 'Blighty' order. I really think he knew he was sinking but he was setting an example of what most British officers do. I think that if I had stayed there I should have broken down. It was getting dusk and I had to be getting back.

As I went back I noticed that the German I took the watch off was no longer in agony. A bayonet was still sticking through his heart, pinning him to the ground. Cruelty had to be met by cruelty – his kind of thing no longer shocked me – I was getting too used to it – it was getting an everyday occurrence.

It was now practically dark and we began to move back quickly. Not a sound was heard and we just followed one another. I did not know who was in the lead. The Officer lasted until we got back. Those who were carrying him laid him on the side of the road – their own lives were too valuable to drag a dead man about, no matter who he was. I wished we could have buried him, but there was not sufficient time.

We went down a long dark lane when machine gun firing was heard from the direction we had just left. No doubt the Boche meant attacking us again in the dark and had found out we were missing. I dread to think what would have happened had we stayed where we were.

Someone evidently anticipated something when they moved us on this night.

We kept on walking and walking. I was about fed up with tramping about.

I turned to ask Bill if I should help him with the Lewis Gun when to my surprise I found he had not got it. I then glanced across to the two fellows who carried the ammunition and also found that they had not got it or any pans either. What had happened?

"Here, catch hold of your rifle," said Bill. "The b----- thing went wrong or something got jammed so I lost it coming along."

"Where's the ammunition gone?" I asked. I hardly knew what else to say.

"We only had a pan and a half left. What's the good of that. They went with the gun."

I was silent and did not know what to say.

"You want to carry a blasted gun all over France what's no good – the sod weighed a ton," Bill said.

I pressed Bill to tell me what he had done with the gun and eventually he told me that he had thrown it in a pond which we crossed over by a plank just before we came into the lane.

"Oh! well, it's gone now and no good worrying over such little matters," said Bill.

"I am really glad, at the bottom of my heart, that we have got rid of it," I said.

No one knew that we were supposed to have the gun, only that Officer and he was now dead, so no questions would be asked.

Eventually we halted and we were going to spend the night in some works which appeared to be cement works. It was no use hunting for straw so we simply threw ourselves down on the cold, hard cement floor and went off to sleep.

CHAPTER IX

BILL'S PICNIC AT BAILLEUL

DAYLIGHT came. Someone woke up. 'Jerry' had been shelling heavily in the night but no one in this room had heard him – all were dead beat. My eyes nearly refused to open and I do not know how I did feel – I was footsore, my back felt as if it would break, dirty, muddy, my shirt was full of lice and I felt as if they would eat me away.

Rations came up later in the morning – three to a loaf this time. I thought that perhaps it would be a bit better next time when a few more of us were killed. Maybe then it would be two to a loaf. We had nothing to drink. I wondered when we had a cup of tea last. The only water we could find was out of the brook. That was better than the other muddy stuff. The day passed slowly along and nothing was seen of the Enemy until late in the afternoon when their great grey masses were seen closing in on us – we had orders to retire at nightfall and we were truly thankful.

That night we slept in a barn just outside Bailleul – which appeared to be a large town. The following morning a few more troops joined us – many of these were Duke of Wellingtons.

We were going to try to hold that town. Many shell holes were in evidence on the outskirts and we took shelter in these. I believe this was about the 14th or 15th April – a week since his last great attack had commenced. What a week! It seemed like an eternity – it was nothing more that Hell upon earth.

We were in a large shell hole with three more fellows – two privates and a Sergeant. Another day had passed away and a few rations came up. This time water to drink came with them in petrol cans. The can we got hold of appeared to contain as much petrol as water – it was terrible to drink but we were glad to get something wet between our lips.

Night time crept over us again – there were no barns to sleep in this time. The only roof we had were the stars and we lay in that rotten shell hole, the bottom of which contained about a foot of dirty water and the sides were slippery with mud; consequently we had difficulty in keeping out of the water. As it was we continually slipped down, our boots getting full of water. God only knew how our feet must be – I had not had a dry foot for over a week. Bill said that if he could stick it long enough the 'treatment' would cure his rheumatic knee. A Corporal and two men belonging to the Red Cross section were in the next shell hole to the one we were in – only about eight or nine yards away.

Verey lights began to appear and a Lewis Gun about a hundred yards away on our right began to fire. It seemed as though things were again becoming lively – the Boche began to shell the town, also his machine guns began to get busy again. Things were now very hot – the old b----- was coming for us in the dark – rifle and machine gun duels were taking place between us. The enemy were not far away when an egg bomb came over.

"Where the Hell did that one come from?" I said.

A party of Germans were in the shell hole just in front of us. We did not see them get in so they must have crawled along very carefully before one of us spotted them. I began to wish we had got our Lewis Gun back. Bill and one of the Wellingtons each threw a bomb over and that certainly quietened them. The Devils would know if one of these dropped in their hole. The machine gun fire on our right was very heavy and on the left many egg bombs were heard mixed with the heavier explosion of the Mills. Many rifles could also now be heard. So far the enemy in front of us had given us no chance to have a shot at them. They were as cunning as monkeys. A Verey light comes over us followed by a few egg bombs which were responsible for someone being badly wounded on our left.

"Stretcher bearer," some one shouted. With that the Corporal and one of his men came out of their hole carrying a stretcher. Egg bombs began to come over again, the enemy no doubt having sighted the movement and we then threw a few more Mills bombs over.

"We hit the old sods then. Hark at that one kicking up," said Bill as he sent one more over which burst just before it hit the ground.

"I shouldn't be surprised if that one had not finished them for good," he continued.

By this time the Corporal and his man had gained our shell hole. The Corporal shouted to the other man they left behind in the other hole to come over.

Again we heard someone call for help.

"Are you coming over, you coward?" shouted the Corporal madly. "Are you coming – this is your last chance?"

"No," came the reply.

"Alright! You shan't." He made no more to do but he picked up one of our Mills bombs and dropped it over. The usual explosion followed then came silence.

I think everyone was too fed up to take any notice of this dreadful action or perhaps the situation was too desperate to worry over such a trifle as one more man getting killed but nevertheless the fact remains that there was one of our own men deliberately killed by one of his fellow countrymen – murdered in cold blood by one of his comrades. Could anyone accuse the Corporal of such an action? No, for he could not have been sane or he would never have done such a thing. He was only like a good many others – he was going mad – his brain could no longer stand the horrible sights, the continual firing of guns, the enormous amount of suffering, hunger and starvation. Eventually the Corporal and his man crept out and disappeared in the darkness.

Machine guns and bombs were still making a terrible noise, but the party of 'Jerries' were very quiet indeed.

As the night passed away so the firing ceased and when morning came we found that the Boche had gone back a little under cover of darkness. This was a second check on this sector, and so we lay when the cold dawn broke in this rotten shell hole. "Stand To" occupied several hours, but nothing happened. Our fellows began to creep from one shell hole to another to have a talk and see if anything was heard about rations. However, time went along and no rations came our way – I could not see how any could be obtained as the Boche had us covered and it would have been suicide to attempt to send rations up to us. We might get them in the dark, it looked as though we had got to stop here without food again. Everybody began to grumble. The Sergeant suggested that we get out and go through the 'Jerries' which were just in front of us in that shell hole.

"There's four or five of 'em, I know," he said, "and they are bound to have plenty of black bread."

"Who says."

"Do you think they are dead?" someone asked.

We all thought our last two bombs must have quietened them and besides nothing was heard of them after that.

Things certainly were very quiet just at this moment. It appeared safe for us to risk it – not a 'Jerry' in sight.

We all slowly crawled towards that hole, the Sergeant leading. We had bombs handy in case we needed them and upon reaching the edge looked in. Empty! We could hardly believe our eyes as we had naturally expected to find four or five dead Germans. We knew our Mills had done some damage as we heard the Boche cry out as though several were badly hurt. There was plenty of evidence to prove that they had been there. We observed that they had been doing a bit of digging at the bottom of the hole. They appeared to have been pulling earth from the side and placing it in the bottom. At first it looked as though they had done this to cover the water which must have been at the bottom. The Sergeant fixed his bayonet and poked the ground.

"Thought so," he said, "there's a 'Jerry' buried here."

As it was not much trouble we decided to unearth him and we soon took away sufficient earth for a pair of legs to show – he had only about six inches of soil over him. We got hold of his legs and gave a pull and had him clear. He was one of the party we had killed in the night but showed no signs of being knocked about. What made the Germans bury their pal so quickly? If this was a general thing they certainly showed more respect and consideration for their dead than we did.

We had a very strange find on this 'Jerry.' He had a gold cross quite thirty inches long by about one and a half feet wide doubled over in three parts under his tunic. No doubt it had come from some church – nearly all the French churches contained these gold crosses or crucifixes in glass cases. I wonder what tale this one could have told – it must have been very valuable. However the Sergeant took possession of this, no doubt with a view to try and get it to 'Blighty' on his next leave.

The next thing for us to do was to get back to our shell hole – we were all about starving.

"Blimey! What about a sausage and mash in Lockharts now and a pint of the best," said Bill.

"Shut up, put a sock in it – what about if we go back into the town and have a look round?" someone else said.

The Sergeant thought this a good idea and Bill was highly delighted.

We were about to move when word came along to say that all of us were falling back on to the town, but it had got to be done quickly.

We soon found ourselves in the town. The town of Bailleul I believe was sixteenth century or perhaps even earlier and of fair size. I do not know quite what the population was. There were many splendid homes of merchants and burgers, a large market-place and a fine hotel with a bell shaped tower, and in a few short hours this fine old town was a mass of ruins and the streets littered with British and German dead. As we reached a fairly large building several of the troops beckoned us to them.

"Hey! mate, do you want some grub – if so, be quick," one of them said. If the whole German Army had fallen on top of us we should not have been more surprised. We immediately went up to the party.

"Go inside – get what you want quickly – she's going up shortly," we were told. It was a large dump of provisions, and the Royal Engineers had mined it – the stuff could not be got away, so rather than let it fall in 'Jerry's' hands they were blowing it up. We hurried inside and nearly fainted at the sight – I began to think it was all a dream. There were stacks and stacks of tinned fruit; strawberries, apricots, peaches, mixed fruit. We were simply mesmerized. In another part of the building were stacks of tobacco and cigarettes by the million – biscuits, not the hard Army issue but good sweet biscuits wrapped in the usual covers. Surely we must be in heaven I thought to myself – bread in plenty.

"Good lor' Bill, hold me up – the smell is getting me down," I said. Bill lost no time – he soon got to work. He found two large sacks and filled one up with cigarettes, cigars and matches. Tens of thousands of them we got in that sack. The other one we filled with bread, biscuits and tins of fruit, but when we came to pick this one up it was so heavy that it would require two men to carry it. It nearly broke our hearts to have to take a lot of the tinned stuff out again.

Bill had another brain wave – he pressed the cigarettes down in my sack and got eight more tins of strawberries in. The place was full of excited, starving troops, any article that would hold anything was soon put in use. Nearly everyone lit a large cigar and the place was full of smoke. Who worried about 'Jerry' now? No one. Food was there in plenty and that was all anyone seemed to care. Everyone took away more than they could carry comfortably, let alone what they could eat. I thought what a lot of fools we were laying in those cold wet holes facing the Boche with no food when there were all these eatables about.

"Hurry up all of you," a soldier on the door shouted. "Get what you want and give the others outside a chance."

I had to help Bill to get his sack on his back – mine was much larger but lighter. The Sergeant and another two had theirs in boxes.

What we were going to do with all the stuff and where we were going we little knew or cared – all that was in our mind was that we intended to have a solid meal and a smoke. The cigarettes we had seemed as though they would last for ever.

We struggled up the street behind the crowd. Bill was staggering all over the road under the weight of his load. I had his rifle which eased him a little. Thank goodness we had not far to go – we turned down a side street and went into the cellars of a large building which looked like a church. Here we found the place full of weary troops. Some were eating, some sleeping and the others smoking. We dropped down and commenced to eat – never in my life have I eaten so much. We opened tin after tin of strawberries with our bayonets and ate them with bread. How much we consumed it would be hard to say but in any case our stomachs were full. After our glorious meal we smoked a cigar. What a contrast to a few hours ago!

The place was very dark but a sackful of flares were brought up from the dump which soon improved matters. The Boche commenced to shell the town heavily – but who troubled about that? Let him shell! Let him do what he likes – we would have wanted a bit of hitting in this cellar.

Bill lay on the floor fast asleep with the cigar hanging out of his mouth, his head on the sack of tinned stuff which was tied up at the end. Bill did not mean losing anything while he was asleep. Suddenly a tremendous explosion was heard. It shook the very ground on which we were – I assumed that it was the end of that dump.

I soon went to sleep and was quite unconscious of all that was going on.

Where the troops who were supposed to be defending the town were I did not know but here in this huge cellar several hundred soldiers lay fast asleep, all quite unconcerned about 'Jerry.' This night as Bill put it, "It was not a bad war now 'Jerry' allowed you to have a little sleep."

There was not a guard on the door of this church nor was there one in the street so that had the enemy known we could all have easily been taken prisoners or murdered on a wholesale scale whichever they had chosen to do, but all were too weary to trouble over any possible danger.

During my peaceful sleep I dreamed that everything was quiet and peaceful, everything seemed warm and tender. I was in my own bed again, back in my own home. I saw food – food was everywhere, the choicest luxuries that money could buy – my mother brought my breakfast up to me in bed – ham and eggs for my breakfast with coffee – but then, it was only a dream and I awoke, forcibly awakened by Bill.

There was pandemonium reigning – in the uncertain light of the flares I could see men rushing their equipment on – two officers were going round giving all who lay asleep a kick to wake them up.

"Get out all of you and line up in the street and he quick – 'Jerry' is in the town," one of them shouted at the top of his voice.

I was still half asleep and could hardly realize where I was for the moment. We went outside – some of us almost walking in our sleep, not forgetting to take with us our sacks of food and cigarettes.

"What the Hell have you got there?" one of the Officers said to me as I was passing with the sack on my back.

"Food," I said.

"Good lord, it looks as if you've got enough stuff to feed the whole army for a month."

Up came Bill with his sack which was much larger.

"Hullo! another Grub merchant? Ah! well you better hang on to it a little longer – we are only going into the main street," the Officer said to Bill.

The Officers marched us a few hundred yards down another street and we went into houses in parties of five, six or seven and were told to be quiet and to be sure to keep our eyes open as 'Jerry' was thought to be somewhere in the town.

"Oh! blast 'Jerry' if he would only let us get a little sleep he could go to Hell," said the Sergeant.

The enemy had been shelling heavily while we slept so we were told. It can easily be imagined how tired we were when we slept through all the noise of the bursting shells. The shells which were now dropping farther into the town sounded terrifying at night. They seem to come with so much more fury than in the day time. Buildings and houses could be heard crashing to the ground.

Daylight came and of course the usual look round had to take place. We found that we were in a fairly large house which was richly furnished. We made our way upstairs and in one of the bedrooms found a full sized bed made up with beautiful white sheets. Oh! the irony of it all. Here we stood, hardly knowing how to keep our eyes open and a bed staring us in the face. In the other bedrooms no beds were erected. After a little discussion between us we decided that three of us should sleep in the bed for two hours while the other three kept watch and then change over. The Sergeant had a watch so we should know when the two hours were up. We tossed up with a penny to see which three should go to bed first and our luck happened to be right in. The Sergeant, Bill and myself won the first two hours. We went into the bedroom and the Sergeant handed over his watch to the three who were to keep a look out.

"Ten minutes to five. Call us at ten minutes to seven," he said, "and mind you, no messing about."

We stood our rifles up against the wall and just took off a portion of our equipment. We kept our gas masks on in case they were needed and we dare not take off too much of our clothing in case we had to shift quick.

We were just about to get into bed when we remembered the sacks downstairs.

"Wouldn't be safe to let them remain too far away from us," Bill remarked. "There's always somebody ready to knock things off."

We went downstairs and brought back with us the two sacks – when we got into the bedroom again the Sergeant was already in bed – his great muddy boots sticking out of the bottom. Bill got in the middle and I on the outside – it was a tight squeeze but we managed to get in alright.

What a sight we must have looked. Three of us in a bed covered with clean linen and there we were covered in mud up to our necks and never had a shave since goodness know when. Six muddy boots stuck out of the bottom. The bedclothes were soon a different colour but these mere details did not worry us and the three of us soon fell asleep.

It did not appear as though we had been in bed more than a minute or two when we were woke up –however we had had our agreed two hours.

Things had been fairly quiet, one shell dropped about ten houses up from here and knocked a few of our chaps out but we did not hear anything.

The second bed party went for their rest while we put our kit on and go downstairs, taking our sacks with us. The Sergeant offered to stay behind a minute to tuck them up. A lot of noise was being made next door. Several shots were heard so we went to see what was the matter. We saw that six or seven soldiers were round a safe. I could see at a glance that the room was used as an office which appeared to be of the Insurance business. They had dragged the safe out of the corner of the room and placed it in the middle and fired four or five revolver shots at the lock. Three fellows were forcing the door with their bayonets. Eventually they forced the door and excitement and speculation ran high but they were sadly disappointed for the safe merely contained papers and deeds which were all, of course, in the French language – the safe was ransacked and the floor of the room covered with various documents. They had been trying to open this safe ever since daylight without any reward for the labour.

After the excitement was over we went back to our own house and had another meal. Time was slipping on and it would soon be our turn again to have another lie down I thought when a sharp burst from a Lewis Gun just across the street brought the three of us to the window to see what was going on. We found that it was two more Portugeuse who had been mistaken for Germans. One was killed instantly but the other escaped unharmed. So many incidents of this nature had taken place that it made one wonder why ever they should wear a similar uniform to that of the enemy. Our chaps did not like the lousy devils – they did not appear as though they washed more than once a year, even when things were normal. The remaining Portugese hurried on up the street as quickly as he could and when he got to the corner of the turning we went down last night he turned round and fired at one of our chaps in the next house, wounding him in the arm. He bolted down the street with half a dozen of the Duke of Wellingtons after him. He was soon captured and brought back. What could they do to him? They could not understand what he said. They pushed him along the passage of the house into the street and just as he was about to leave one of our troops pulled the pin out of a Mills Bomb, quickly puts it in his large overcoat pocket, gives him a push and slammed the door everybody at the same time running into the kitchen. The result is obvious, this Potugese was literally blown to pieces. He had no doubt done wrong but nevertheless he was a human being and was fighting on our side. One can only assume that the reason for him shooting one of our men was because of the tragic circumstances under which he lost his pal. An Officer came round and enquired what had been going on, but as usual no one admitted knowing anything of what had taken place. He did however order that the corpse was to be removed from the door in order that people could get in and out of the house without being impeded. What a War!

Into this town came a member of the East Lancashire Regiment whose battalion had just come from Passendale way. He told us that it was Hell. Nothing but mud and pineapples and dirty Portuguese. Photographs of the Portuguese were supplied to our troops at this point in order that they would not be mistaken, but they were of little use as no one could distinguish between a German and one of these dirty devils at a distance of about five hundred yards – this being the reason for a lot of them being killed. Another soldier informed us that the Portuguese ran away whenever a shell was fired and then fired into the backs of the British. Another Tommy went farther by saying that he had seen them with the Boche. I would not like to confirm this as the absolute truth but there certainly were some funny things happening whenever these troops were in the front line.

Our three companions who had been in bed came downstairs – they said they could not sleep with all the blasted noise going on. We took advantage of this and got into bed again but we were hardly settled down when an Officer came up and finding the Sergeant and Bill and I in bed said, "What in the Hell do you think you are up to? What Regiment do you belong to? Do they allow you to sleep all day? Get downstairs quick!" We threw the sheet back and he saw the stripes of the Sergeant.

"Sergeant, I am ashamed of you – you ought to know better. What explanation have you to offer?"

Our Sergeant could tell at a glance he was new to the game and had just come out to France.

"Blimey, when you've been out here as long as me you'll want a sleep. That's about the first sleep for over a week."

"Have you lost all your manners? I am entitled to 'Sir' when you address me. I have been out here a month now and I think most of you fellows have forgotten what you learnt when in England. I am used to folks jumping to it quickly when I speak so please remember that. Now go downstairs and set the other fellows a better example."

We went downstairs then the Officer said, "Sergeant, bring half a dozen men to go for rations. Get enough for fifty. My runner will go with you to show you where to go."

Off we went. We had only to go over the old square where many shells had fallen. Three sets of limbers, each with two horses, all lay here knocked out. In the middle of two dead horses lay their dead driver. We ultimately arrived at our destination where many others were drawing rations. The Sergeant walked inside and obtained rations for sixty – ten more than we were told and beckoned us in to pick them up. Thirty loaves – hard issue biscuits, eight pots of jam, some margarine and four petrol cans full of water. The Officer told the Sergeant to distribute them. Of course all in our party had a loaf extra, also jam and margarine.

Shells were dropping in the town much faster but strange to relate no British Artillery answered back. What ever had happened to them? Towards mid-day there was a considerable increase in the machine gun fire and bomb explosions could be heard in several streets away. I anticipated that somebody was getting it a bit thick. Two or three of our fellows came running round the corner of the street. We called them in. What tales they had to tell. 'Jerry' is in the street which they had just come from and in a good many cases in the same houses. "There's thousands of them," they said. Hand to hand fighting was taking place and sniping from one window to another. Everything up that street is Hell.

"He'll have the lot of them if they ain't careful," one chap said. The noise and the uproar got louder and louder. He was in the next street now. The German shells were falling fast but short – they were falling in their own ranks – German soldiers losing their lives by their own gun fire, but what did that seem to matter to their countless thousands? British troops could be seen running back at the top end of our street. Those who could get away now were lucky. Oh! I was about sick of it all – he would be here in about a minute now. They swooped round the corner of the street – just like a wave of human masses. We emptied our rifles into them but it was just like putting a man on a railway line to stop an express train – as soon as one b----- dropped two more took their place. On they came – nothing on earth could hope to stop such a mad rush. We all went through the house out of the back door down the garden over a high wall. When I was on top of the wall I suddenly wondered where Bill was and when I looked back I saw he was struggling with the sack of cigarettes.

"The sods ain't gonna have these," he shouted down the garden as he caught my eye.

I helped him over with his baggage by getting hold of one end of the sack and he the other and throwing it over the wall.

We ran like madmen let out of an asylum – there were hundreds of us, each one wondering whether we would get out of the town alive or whether we would run right into the enemy again. We kept on, and were soon on the outskirts of the town the whole crowd of us continuing down the road. No doubt by this time the Boche was in complete possession of the town. Blast him, I thought – he has all that food again and all those extra rations – all those tins of fruit, may they choke him!

"Hell of a War this is. Why can't we have as many men as he has, and treat him like he is treating our chaps?" I said

CHAPTER X

THE GOLDEN CROSS

ABOUT half way between Bailleul and St. James La Pell our fellows were digging in. A few soldiers every seventy or eighty yards apart were digging a trench. A load of shovels lay on the road. We took one each and made our way across several fields until we came to another large farm building. The Sergeant had a look round and decided to stay in this building. I noticed there was plenty of straw about. The majority of the British troops would not have anything to do with buildings if they could possibly avoid it as they were believed to be so much more dangerous than the open country, their reason being that the Boche took his range by them for his Artillery. We had risked it before so we intended doing it again. As the Sergeant remarked, we could get a bit of comfort here and we could easily clear out if the shelling became too bad. With that we settled ourselves down in the clean wheat straw – the only fly in the ointment being we had nothing to eat. The pump in the yard could supply us with plenty of water, which was something to be thankful for.

The remainder of the day passed by uneventfully and when night came four of us slept while two kept a sharp look out. However, the night passed by quietly and we all succeeded on getting a certain amount of sleep. We were all very restless owing to the lice which we carried about with us. I felt like burning my shirt, but the nights were too cold.

Morning came and there was every indication of it being a beautifully sunny day. We immediately had a look round as soon as it was daylight to see if there were any eatables about. We went to the chaps in the first trench but they were unable to give us supplies – they were short themselves. We decided that it was useless trying to obtain food and so we went back to the straw and lay down and rested, but it was only for a brief period as about eleven o'clock the enemy commenced to shell us as hard as ever. One shell dropped close to the building – we knew that the best thing to do now was to clear out as quickly as possible as it would not be long before the entire structure was demolished.

We seized our shovels and went back into a small grass field and began to dig in as hard as we could go. In about an hour we had got down about three feet in the soft ground and were then obliged to cease as water was appearing. We had to content ourselves with what we had been able to do. By this time the shelling somewhat quietened, but not as much as we would have liked. We dare not go back to that wheat straw as we felt that we were much safer where we were.

A 'Jerry' airplane put in an appearance, flying low. He came right over our trench and for us to let him go without trying to bring him down was too much of a temptation. We could just see the pilot and we all let drive. Shot after shot was fired at him as he circled round. He came back again over our trench but this time he was flying a little higher and as he passed over us he dropped several green lights and then made off towards the German lines. To us this appeared very strange. What a pity we could not hit him.

We soon found out what the purpose of his visit was. The green lights were the range or signal for a certain Battery to fire and by God didn't they fire. The shells dropped everywhere in that small field. We all crouched in that shallow trench our faces touching the ground. Harder and harder they came until I began to wonder whether or not Hell was upon earth. There were now many shrapnel bursts coming over and we could hear the shrapnel falling on the ground with a thud.

What fools we were to have interfered with that airplane. I would not fire at another one for a day or two after this.

The shelling never ceased for a minute and the grass field was literally being ploughed up – shells dropped everywhere – just in front – just over and one on the end of the trench where I and the Sergeant lay. As this shell dropped the thought flashed through my mind that this was the end, but then, no, "I was alright" I thought as the last clod of soil fell over me. What a dreadful sensation. As this shell burst I felt as though I must be hit and my end had come as it had done to many others.

This shelling kept on for about another twenty minutes and not once did it stop during the whole of the time, but everything comes to an end sometime. I looked up and saw what a contrast that field was to what it was before the shelling had commenced. Twenty minutes ago it was a beautiful small grass paddock – now it was a wilderness all churned up. I glanced at the Sergeant. "Good Lor'!" I exclaimed. He had not moved and I saw that blood was running down his face. I found that a piece of shrapnel as big as a walnut had entered the top of his tin hat and obviously enough had lodged in his brain, killing him instantly. He only lay about two yards away from me and I never heard a sound. We lifted him out of the trench and laid him on the top.

"No it's no good. He's as dead as mutton," I said to Bill. I had thought life might not have been quite extinct.

The four of us then got back into the trench, where we said we would decide what to do next. I was in favour of moving and they all agreed. We had all had sufficient of the enemy's shelling, but where were we to go? We did decide, however, to move farther back and dig in again in a fresh place. We got out of the trench to move off. The Sergeant lay there dead, his eyes wide open as if he were looking at us. It made me shudder.

"We can't leave him like this. Let's bury him somewhere," I said to my companions.

We agreed to bury him and decided that his grave should be the trench which he himself had helped to dig. Little did he think when he was digging that trench that he was digging his own grave. I helped to pick him up – what a weight he was! He was already getting stiff.

"Oh, be quick. Let's get this over!" I exclaimed.

One of my companions took off his wrist watch and also took his wallet. He promised to send them home if he could get through this lot himself. We placed him in the bottom of the trench and commenced to cover him with soil when someone remembered the Gold Cross. He jumped down, undid his tunic and took possession of it.

"Blast it – I don't want it. I don't like the thing. This is the second dead man the cross has been on in the last two days," I said.

"Leave it on him, the thing will only bring you bad luck," someone said.

"No, it's no good," I said as he took the cross. He evidently intended taking it and when he got out of the trench he put it under his tunic while we finished burying the Sergeant.

We had seen plenty of dead these last few days but the latest loss of our Sergeant seemed to upset us more than ever.

"Come on – let's get away, the place is getting on my nerves," I said as we moved away, but back again we had to go once more. This time for the sack of cigarettes. We went into the next field and got into a dyke. How uncanny it seemed without the Sergeant. We were hungry, wet and utter gloom and despair was stamped over all of us – even Bill was affected.

The Enemy once more commenced their devilish shelling but this time were spreading over a bigger area.

Bill and I decided to walk back a little way into St. James La Pell before it was dark as it was now getting late in the afternoon. We intended to see if we could lay our hands on some food. The other two stayed behind. We reached the village in a few minutes and found the place full of French troops. We walked into the first house we came to and found it packed with them – all spotlessly clean and many of them playing cards. I noticed Bill's face brighten up when he saw this.

Others were cleaning their rifles. When I saw this I looked at ours and they gave me the impression that they would never be clean again and with us in our terrible condition we formed a striking contrast to them. They swarmed round us and we soon made them understand what we wanted. We did not look like getting any food until we could tell them that we could exchange cigarettes for food. We parted with ten packets for a large flat brown loaf and some grease of some sort. Had we given them more cigarettes we could have obtained a further supply of bread but as we had not more with us we promised to come back again later that night. We stepped towards a card party in whom we were interested. How long it seemed since last I played. Bill wanted to borrow a few francs to try his luck but I did not agree. In any case I wanted something to eat and our companions were waiting for us. We made our way back and 'Jerry' was still busy shelling. We reached the Dyke where we left our comrades and we were horror-stricken with the sight that confronted us. The dyke had been blown in – one of our pals lay there dead, he had been hit in the stomach and half his insides were hanging out. The other one was not to be seen but a trail of blood towards the road showed us that although wounded, he had made his way somewhere, but where we had not the faintest idea. It was no use worrying. Which one was killed we could not say, as the one who lay there was covered in blood and unrecognisable. We had another look at him. How ghastly he appeared.

"No, I am not sure which one it is," I said to Bill. "Good Lord, look, Bill," I continued as I pointed towards him. I had just noticed that Gold Cross sticking out from where he was wounded. This was the third man to die in the last four days who was in possession of the Gold Cross. I wondered if there was anything in it. I certainly was becoming very superstitious. It was very queer and I am sure I never had such a feeling before.

"It's that cross. Yes, it's that cross," I kept saying. "Let's get away from it all. No. We couldn't desert, that's the coward's way."

It was nearly dark and we still stood there and I could not keep my eyes off the end of that cross.

"Let's go somewhere Bill, I've had enough."

Bill did not intend moving until the sack of cigarettes were found. Eventually he found them half covered with soil where the dyke got 'pushed in.'

We decided to go back to where the French troops were and try to spend the night there and then see what morning brought forth. On our way I could see that cross – then the dead 'Jerry' whom we took it off –then our Sergeant and now this chap. I wondered where the German got it from – perhaps he, too, got it off a dead man.

"Thank goodness!" I said when we arrived with the French. It was good to be in company even if we did not understand much what they were saying.

We got rid of twenty more packets of smokes and took bread in exchange. It was by this time quite dark and a lamp was lit showing a good light. All the windows were covered with blankets to keep the light from shining out in the street.

Card playing was in full swing while Bill continually worried me for a loan to enable him to join in a game. However I decided to lend Bill the money and also to have a game myself as it would tend to take my mind off the horrible time we had just passed through. While we played cards everything was fairly quiet.

We soon found that the French idea of playing cards was entirely different to the way we played in England and we were at a great disadvantage in not being able to understand what the French troops were saying. In about two hours we were both 'broke' – we were inclined to think that the money was taken away from us unfairly. Ah, well we had had our food and Bill was satisfied!

A French Officer came in and gave some orders but he did not notice Bill and I lying in the corner of the room. The French troops were obviously feeling tired and first one and then another of them would lay on the floor and in about ten minutes the light was turned out and the place was in darkness. Nothing unusual came to our notice with the exception that, unlike us, they had two guards outside.

Morning came and at daybreak everyone was about – many French troops had come in during the night and we learnt that they had taken over the whole sector here and that the few British troops who were left had gone back in the night, but no one appeared to know or even care where they had gone.

"Well of all the blasted things this makes the second time we've lost everyone," I said to myself. "Ah, well I suppose most of it is our own fault!"

"A night under a roof is a b----- sight better than laying in a trench half full of water," Bill remarked.

We had a look round and could see nothing but French troops – thousands of them. They were digging trenches which connected up with each other and it appeared to us that they were going to put up a determined stand. Thank goodness 'Jerry' would not have it all his own way now. With all these troops it appeared as though they stood a sporting chance with the enemy. Everything seemed so different to the way we had been fighting the last few days with our handful of men.

We decided to go back to the Farm and found that several batteries of French Seventy five's had come up and more troops were behind them. They came up only just in time to relieve the remains of a weary army of men. This retreat could not have gone on much longer – flesh and blood could not have stood it. A few more of our troops came up and amongst them was one of our battalion. We enquired where the others had gone but they did not know. They appeared very tired and weary and were glad to sit down and rest. French troops were continually going in and out – activity and excitement ran high. More French troops were expected and they hoped to be able to hold the 'Boche.' Next a party of French soldiers came in and they appeared pleased over something. It transpired that they had been out searching for anything they could find and they had discovered that gold cross.

"Blast the thing – we shall never see the end of it," I said.

It was covered with blood and we knew whose blood it was. They wiped the blood off it and gathered round speaking quickly and loud. They no doubt considered that they had a good find. This wholesale pilfering of the dead was very rife. It did not matter which country one was fighting for or even what side you were on the dead were always robbed by the living.

We told them of what we knew of that cross and what had happened but they were determined to stick to it. They then went out of the house by the back door and that was the last we saw of the cross, but I could not help but wonder if the then present owner ever shared the fate of the previous owners.

Now began one of the biggest tasks we had yet encountered and that was to go back and find our battalion. Bill and I and our new pal 'Chester' Weetley started out to go somewhere to be guided to wherever fate guided us. We had not the faintest idea where we were going but set out with the sole idea of walking somewhere in the hope that we should come across the remainder of our battalion.

We kept on walking – how long and how many miles God only knew. We must have walked a tremendous distance as our feet were getting sore – we were tired and beginning to feel the effects of hunger and starvation. Fortunately we had a few cigarettes and though many were spoiled through being crushed they kept us going. Chester related that he had a small pig in the sack which he was carrying on his back. It was only about five weeks old and what he intended doing with it I did not know but he was an old 'sweat' and knew what he was doing like all the troops who had been in France for a considerable period. Time in this Hell learnt us troops lots of 'dodges' and the longer one was in France the more artful and crafty one seemed to be. Everywhere in this sector seemed full of French troops but we eventually came across the headquarters of the Duke of Wellingtons where we stayed the night. After making many enquiries we heard that our battalion was at a certain village. The next day we again set off and after a journey which seemed endless we arrived there only to learn that they had left the previous day. A Battalion of Northumberland Fusiliers were here resting. Our condition was appalling. What a filthy state we were in – our clothes all muddy and torn in many places – boots sadly needed repairing and a fortnight's growth of beard on our chins. As we walked through the camp our looks caused more than usual interest to be taken in us. One or two of the troops here began to get impudent and were trying to make fun out of us. They no doubt had only just come out. We resented their attitude and there was every indication of there being a nasty argument when a Captain came along and seeing us soon wanted to know everything about us. We explained our position and he told us to get into Hut Number 10 and he would find out something during the day where our battalion was. We were supplied with a little food. The Captain was not a bad sort.

Bill sold what cigarettes we could spare for five francs and with the money we decided to let him try his luck on the Crown and Anchor Board, where play was in full swing outside Hut Number 9. Bill staked the money while Chester and I stood back looking on.

All Crown and Anchor Boards are alike to Bill – he only stakes the money on his favourite, namely, the 'Mudhook.' His luck appeared to be in as the 'Mudhook' more than held its own. Bill puts six francs on and to our utter amazement it comes up three times in succession and he draws twenty four francs – just Gamblers' luck. A runner then came up and told us that we were wanted down at the Headquarters. We followed him and at the same time counting up the winnings – we now had thirty two francs.

We went into the village and as we passed the first cottage we saw a notice in the window which read, 'Coffee, Eggs and Chips – 1 franc.'

"Good lor' – wait till we come back – we will try those eggs and chips," said Bill.

We eventually reached the Headquarters, which were in a large house in the centre of the village. We were shown in a room where the Captain was sitting at a table. He duly informed us that we were to have a blanket and stay the night and that it would be sometime the next day before we were told where we were to go. We then left to fetch our blankets and when we had done this we hurried to that cottage with only one thought – to have a 'buster' meal. We walked in and quite a pretty M'mselle greets us who we soon made understand that we required coffee eggs and chips and that she is to keep on frying until we tell her to stop. Oh, the smell of those eggs as they were frizzling in the pan! It brings memories of home back to me. Plate after plateful is brought to us to satisfy our ravenous appetite. What was one small egg and a few chips to us starving men? We called a halt as the ninth plateful was given to us. That was the first solid meal we had had for a long time – nine plates each and four cups of coffee. We handed over twenty seven francs in payment which soon knocked a hole in our winnings. Anyhow we still had five francs left which we had started with so we must not grumble.

We picked up our blankets and made our way back to the Huts and when we arrived back there was a Hell of a row in Hut 10. It turned out that two transport soldiers had been fighting – they had been in the village 'on the booze,' one of them apparently had found all the necessary money. Not until they got back did the other one discover his best pair of boots were missing. They had been 'flogged' to finance the 'boozing expedition.' However things quietened down when the Sergeant Major put in an appearance to see what the trouble was and took the names of the culprits.

We now felt in a much better humour after having a substantial meal and this incident amused us immensely – the three of us stood there giggling and the Sergeant Major turned round on us like a madman and wanted to know what we were laughing at. We did not answer him and I believe he would have taken our names had he not seen that we belonged to another 'mob.' He told us in some forceable language to get a shave.

"Got no razor," I answered him.

To this he said he would fit us up and poor Chester had to follow him right back into the village again to fetch the damn thing. I went down to the wash place and 'knocked off' a piece of soap while no one was looking. Bill in the meantime had managed to lose our last five francs on the Crown and Anchor Board so we were all broke again.

Chester arrived back with an old razor which was completely worn out.

Looks like an old issue one – looks like it might have seen service at Mons," I said as I commenced to strop it on the sling of one of our rifles.

Bill agreed to allow Chester to shave him first. Oh, the torture! I could see Bill was going through the Mill with that old blunt razor

"Damn the thing. It's no good at all," Chester said. It was utterly impossible to shave so we had to go without a shave once more.

Chester decided to pull the pig out of the sack and have a look at it. It looked dreadful – covered with blood and pieces of sacking and he began to wonder what he was going to do with it himself now. One of the transport men who was standing by said that if it could be cleaned he could get it down to the cookhouse provided we would allow him to stand in with us when feeding time came along. We took it down to the washhouse and gave it a swill. After this it certainly looked more like a pig. We opened it and cleaned out its insides but the trouble arose how we were to get the bristles off. Bill solved the trouble when he suggested that we shave it with the razor. Chester soaped the pig and shaved it as best as he could. After a lot of trouble and about half a dozen swills under the pump the pig looked in a more presentable condition. Chester and our new comrade took it down the horse lines where the cookhouse was and after a little more squaring down there were told that we could have it sometime the next day.

That night we lay on bare boards with one blanket over us. It was bitterly cold – our bodies were aching and felt as stiff as the boards did themselves. As tired and as worn out as we were, real sound sleep was impossible. We really only lay shivering and dozing until daybreak. Daylight was really welcomed so that I could get up and have a run round to warm myself up a little. Eight o'clock came and we managed to get hold of some hot tea, not too strong and plenty of grease on the top, but nevertheless it was hot – it certainly did seem to go down well – it seemed ages since we last had tea. The others went on parade at nine o'clock so we then had the Hut to ourselves. We felt relieved to be able to have all our equipment off and able to sit down in peace and safety. A lot different to those farms we left a day or two ago. I began to itch again and decide to take my shirt off while I had the opportunity, Bill and Chester deciding to do likewise. What a sight they were – scores of lice were sticking to our shirts down the seams in almost every available atom of space.

"What do you say they are, Bill – Chats?" I said.

"I should think so," he replied.

"My shirt's alive," said Chester.

Mine was just as bad – dozens of the horrible things – all colours, grey, blue and even red. We did nothing but kill the devils for fully an hour.

"Some say a hot iron is the only remedy," Bill said. "But the only sure way is to crack 'em. Why the blasted air must be full of 'em."

I continually went over my shirt and the more I killed the more I seemed to find.

Our trousers and tunics were in just the same condition and when we turned them inside out we found hundreds of the swine – all in the seams – they were so thick that one would have thought there were millions of them. "France must be damn well lousy," I thought to myself.

We killed as many as we possibly could and as we dressed ourselves Chester remarked that there would be just as many again the next day.

As we completed dressing ourselves a soldier looked in the Hut and asked if we required any letters posting.

"Good God!" I said as it suddenly struck me that it was over a fortnight since we had been able to send any letters away. What must Mother think at home with all this fighting going on and not hearing a word? I could picture her in my mind meeting each post and no letter for her from France. I could see the disappointment in her face as she looked through the letters. How she must have suffered, at this moment probably wondering what had happened and obviously anticipating the worst. Little did I dream that only the previous day that a notice appeared in a Northamptonshire evening paper that Private F. Smith was missing and believed killed. The same announcement appeared about Bill in a London paper. There was no need to wonder why our parents were in such a wretched state.

For a few fags we obtained some paper and envelopes off the postman who said that he would call again in twenty minutes after he had been round the other Huts.

We had each just completed our letters when the postman came and in each of those letters was the good news being conveyed to England from 'Somewhere in France.' At least three soldiers were safe and in good health.

I felt relieved when this was done for a load was taken off my mind. My next thoughts were to get back to my battalion so that I could get a letter from home. Home! The very words seemed out of place in this Hell. I suppose we must consider ourselves lucky that we only signed for 'Duration' – there is a hope that we should get home again.

It was now nearly dinner time and the fellows were coming in off parade but we had not heard a word from the Captain about ourselves – there was also no word about that pig.

"Hullo! Here's that transport chap coming now," I said.

"We shall soon get to know something about it now," said Bill.

"Sorry," he said, "the Captain spotted it and made the cook get rid of it. Damn bad luck – that's all it is."

We looked at each other in dismay – it was no use grumbling if things did not go just right. In any case matters could not be too bad, as we were having the same dinner as the others.

So far as the pig is concerned I was not altogether sure about its destiny and I later found out that the transport soldier had 'flogged' it to the Sergeant's mess for three francs.

Late in the afternoon we received orders to proceed to a certain place somewhere in France miles behind the lines and were told to get away as soon as possible as we had a long walk in front of us. Our battalion was expected there this day but if they had not arrived there when we did we were to wait until they did come.

CHAPTER XI

WE REJOIN OUR REGIMENT

WE commenced our journey in search of the battalion to which we belonged. We tramped over main roads, by-roads and lanes for miles and miles. We got tired – the continual walking was monotony in its worst form. We felt as though we were on an endless walk – a tramp which had to be kept up as anxious as we were to rest – we dare not stop in case we missed our battalion.

We passed through several villages – the estaminets were open, all packed with troops drinking and enjoying themselves under strange circumstances. We were thirsty – so thirsty we felt like dying – felt like giving up. We had not a franc between us, Bill being fool enough to lose what little money we had with his persistent gambling.

Something had got to be done – we were on the verge of collapse and we decided that the next 'boozer' we came to we would try to get a drink somehow. It was not long before we came to the next village which had been subject to 'Jerry's' bombardment. The only few French people left were running the estaminet and Red Lamp together. Trade to them must have been good for although no troops were stationed in the village there were always plenty in the district. These few people evidently intended hanging on to the very last in order to keep their business going.

We entered the place and it was packed with troops – English – Canadian – Irish – Scotch. The room was thick with tobacco smoke and we felt as if we should choke as we staggered in. Some of the troops could see what a dreadful condition we were in. We soon made them understand that we required something to drink and as we narrated some of our experiences they supplied us with whatever beverage we desired which was available.

A staircase led from this room to the rooms above and on these stairs stood a queue of men comprising all nationalities – even a lousey 'chink.' They were coming to visit a certain girl who was there. To prove what a terrible trade this is – only one girl was on the premises for this purpose. As one man left the bedroom another one entered and so it went on and on. The Chinaman's turn came and he was treated as all the others were – all were welcome so long as they were able to pay four francs.

This house could not last much longer for as soon as the information reached Headquarters it would be closed down and a notice would appear in the window 'Out of bounds.' The proprietors would then pack up their kit and start a fresh place somewhere else.

The next thing I noticed was the Chinaman coming downstairs and the girl following closely behind. She spoke to the man behind the bar (if it could be called a bar). She was a big coarse Belgian girl and her only attire was a transparent gown. The man to whom she spoke went to the remainder of the queue and told them that the girl had finished business for the day. An argument at once set up and the Frenchman got excited and waved his arms about in the air. There were all appearances of being a nasty row but things quietened down. During this time Bill was trying to 'raise the wind' as we called it when trying to get hold of money. He managed to sell his German revolver for fifteen francs and with the proceeds bought wine. All our money went, but who cared? Nobody. We were getting merry. Chester got noisy and wanted to fight the 'Chink' and did eventually throw him out into the street.

I sold my revolver, but did better than Bill, as I succeeded in obtaining twenty francs for it, so we were financially sound for a little longer at any rate, and we kept on drinking and drinking.

Someone sang a song, accompanied by a mouth organ. There were loud cheers – all were nearly drunk.

Bill was in a lively mood and went to the front to sing a song – he stooped down to hum the tune to the soldier who was playing the mouth organ. He faced the crowd at the same time taking off his tin hat, which by the way, was the first time he had taken it off for about a fortnight. Someone shouted at him and asked if he wanted to borrow a razor – he certainly did not have the music hall appearance, but he was full of wine and did not care for anything or anybody. He sang 'Are you going back to London,' in his half drunken condition, but I must give him credit – he sang well. At the end of his song he was encored and then sang again, this time 'God send you back to me' and so the programme went on until closing time. My twenty francs by this time had nearly all gone and we were practically dead drunk. Chester lost his rifle and although he left it with ours near the door someone 'knocked it off.' He did not care – there were plenty more where that one came from and there was one consolation – it was all the less to carry. In any case, a man did not want to carry much in the condition we were. As we staggered out of this filthy place into the street there were a number of 'Red Caps' about watching us disperse.

We could not remember the name of the place to which we were supposed to be going.

There is no doubt we were in a mess – half drunk and did not know where we were to go – we were as helpless as a child so we sat down on the roadside and rested. I did not think we were far off the camp but at the same time I thought it strange that we did not see any of our chaps in the 'boozer' – in any event we could not report in the condition we were then in. Bill was drunk as a lord, and Chester and I were not much better. Before having the drink we were tired and weary but the wines had livened us up considerably for the brief period we were in the estaminet, but the drink was now telling its tale on us, and we all soon fell asleep.

How long we had been asleep I do not know but something woke me up. Oh, my head! It felt as if it were opening and shutting. I was wet through and no wonder – it was raining in torrents, but for how long it had done so I had not the faintest idea. I looked at Bill and

Chester and they were still sound asleep and lay there as if they had not a care in the world. A soldier with a limber and two horses was coming down the road so I woke up my two comrades. We stopped the driver of the limber and to our astonishment he was a member of our battalion. We jumped on the limber and moved off.

"How far have we to go?" I asked.

"Oh, only about five miles!" he replied. "We are going under canvas – all the tents are up but the chaps don't come in until the early hours of the morning."

"What's the time now? "

"About two o'clock," was the reply.

"Good lor' we have layed there a time, Bill," I said. Bill had not much to say – I could see that the ride was not suiting him and the driver had to pull up twice at Bill's request.

At last we arrived at the camp and it was just about three o'clock. The driver of the limber knew a good deal about the camp and showed us the tent where we could find the Quartermaster Sergeant if we dare wake him up.

"Dare? Who in the Hell's going to stand about for the rest of the night?" snapped Bill. We approached the tent.

"Are you there, sir?" I said meekly.

"Are you there, sir?" I said again, this time in a much louder voice.

"Yes. Who is it?" the reply came.

We told him who we were as we still stand outside the tent.

"Oh, yes! What do you say? Only three of you? C Company? Go and get in any of the tents in the first row from the hedge – the others are expected in sometime about 5.30."

"What about some blankets?" whispered Bill.

"Blankets? I'll give you blankets in the middle of the night. Get out while yer safe," he yelled.

We retired and left him in peace. We stopped at the first tent we came to and undid the flap. Inside we found a yard of clean wheat straw and some ground sheets. We soon got inside and fastened up the flap again and after we had struck a few matches to enable us to have a look round we threw ourselves down in the straw and in a few moments we were fast asleep once again. So far this was the best bed we had had since we came out to France.

It seemed as though no sooner were we asleep and we were awakened.

There was a terrible noise outside – the battalion had arrived and we could hear someone allotting the tents out to the men. One remark we heard was, "Come on, be quick, Woodenheads. Sixteen to a tent and jump to it." And so the row went on and on, then that voice ceased, and just as we thought we were going to have a tent on our own the flap was undone. It transpired that the tent we had got in was reserved for the four Company Sergeant Majors and two of their favourite Sergeants.

In about a minute and a half we were outside again with rifle and gas mask in one hand and our boots in the other, wondering where on earth we were going next. We took what we anticipated as our only chance by making our way to another tent. As each tent had sixteen men in it can easily be imagined that to have three more met with disapproval. However we were allowed in and once more lay down, but this time not on a nice bed of straw such as we had been turned out of – we were unlucky this time – we had to lay on the bare ground but we had to be thankful in getting somewhere to sleep. The only advantage we had was we could keep warm as we were almost sleeping on top of one another. It was now about six o'clock and by eight o'clock we were out and about again. Breakfast was up, consisting of a small piece of fish and tea, bread of course being supplied overnight. We had no bread, and not having a Dixie or a lid had the fish in our hands. In order that we could have some tea we asked the soldier who was rationing this out to leave enough in the bottom of the pot for three so that we could have this when everybody else had finished. Our breakfast merely comprised one small piece of fish and very little greasy tea. In fact there were more tea leaves than tea. While we were sitting there I could see that we were causing a good deal of attention. These troops who we were with had just come out from England and were all smartly equipped, with bright buttons, shining shoes, and spotless in every detail. Some asked where we had been to get in such a condition others wanted to know when we last had a shave and scores of other questions were fired at us. These fellows who had just come from England had not the slightest idea what we had been through and what they might perhaps have to go through themselves. If they had to go through what we did they would understand what it meant to be a soldier in time of war. What a contrast we were to them – covered in mud, worn out shoes were our lot, torn clothes and long beards. There was no need to wonder why they asked us all these questions.

Although with our own battalion there was not one chap amongst them with whom we came out – this was easily explained, the battalion had been made up with new troops to full strength – there is no doubt that it was needed, for out of one thousand two hundred men who went into that wheat field on the 7th of April less than fifty answered the roll call when they were taken out of action a few days after – C Company was completely wiped out and I believe we three were the only survivors.

After breakfast we reported to the Sergeant Major. What a surprise he had when he saw us! Our condition was pitiful. To look at we were like scarecrows one sees in wheat fields to frighten birds away from the corn. Our shoes were worn to pieces, the soles of them being worn into holes, our uniforms were caked in mud from top to bottom, our puttees had gone, our faces were haggard and unshaven, our haunted eyes told their tale – we were tired worn out and footsore – alive with lice – we were complete wrecks. The Sergeant Major could see our coloured stars on the sleeves of our tunics. He knew in a moment that we were just three more soldiers who had been reported missing to drift in from that sector of the British lines where one of the greatest battles in History had been fought.

"What names do you say – Smith, Worthy and Weetley?" he said as he commenced to look the record book up.

He informed us that we had been reported missing and believed killed. He then asked us where we had been, and we told him all. Whilst we stood there Bill whispered, "I wonder where the Sergeant Major was when 'Jerry' came over."

He looked up and said to Bill, "What are you on about?"

"I wonder if you could fit us up with some food; it's been a day since we had any," Bill answered.

"The best I can do is to take you to the Captain."

In a few minutes the three of us were standing at attention in front of Captain Kay. When I say this was a complete surprise to us it can easily be understood, for the last time we saw the Captain was when he came up to us on the morning of April the 7th when the German Army had broken through our front at Armentieres. He too had arrived back safely. He asked us a few questions and smiled. He was a real good sort and a thorough gentleman – fear was unknown to him. He was in charge of C and D Companies when the Boche attacked, the battalion at that time being a Captain short but was now at full strength and he was now only in charge of C Company. Captain Kay who had brought his own chargers and servant out with him, when in private life was a country squire, and racehorse owner, having a big estate in the Midlands consisting of several thousands of acres. He turned to the Sergeant Major and said, "See that these men are fitted up with food – let them go down this afternoon with the limbers and get a complete outfit."

"Yes, sir," was the reply.

The Captain dismissed the Sergeant Major and told the three of us to stay. When he had gone he commenced to talk to us as though he was only a Private. He wanted to know what we did at so-and-so and how we got away from those railway lines, and didn't his eyes gleam with pleasure when we told him how we had shot those five 'Jerries' from the farmhouse windows.

"Good," he said, "I only wish I had been with you."

We told him all, at any rate all we dare. When he dismissed us he left the impression on us that if needed we would follow him through thick and thin.

We called at the cookhouse for our rations, the Sergeant Major having made all the necessary arrangements. What a difference when you are in favour! This time we happened to be on the right side.

We received one whole loaf each, a pot of jam for two and two packets of issue cigarettes and a tin of bully-beef if we wanted it. If we had been in the line the amount of food which each one of us had this day would have had to have done for four men and perhaps five.

That evening saw the three of us in new clothes and a complete new outfit, and in addition a pay day. Of course we always managed to 'lose' our pay books – they told too many tales. A young Second Lieutenant paid us out this night. He sat at a little table with all the money in front of him. The usual amount for each soldier was ten to fifteen francs. If more was required it meant asking the Officer if it was possible to have extra making the excuse that you wanted to send home for some particular article. He would then probably instruct you to stand on one side until the whole of the company is paid out and if there was then any cash to spare would see how it worked out, and strange to say there practically always was a surplus and furthermore it seemed peculiar that the same little party always stayed behind to see what surplus there might be. Bill and I always used to be included. This night there was a considerable amount of money left over and one soldier asked for thirty francs extra, which he received without hesitation whatever.

Bill's turn came next and he coolly asked for Fifty francs.

The Officer looked up and said, "Let's look at your pay book"

"Sorry, Sir, 'Jerry' had it in the last do." Bill replied. That was always a good excuse.

However Bill succeeded in obtaining his fifty francs and a new pay book. I went through the same procedure and also succeeded in obtaining fifty francs. Never before during the whole of the time we had been in the Army had we been so well off – brand new clothes and sixty five francs each. We intended to visit the nearest village and have a beano. We learnt later that no sooner had we received our pay and got out of sight when the Commanding Officer put in an appearance and wanted all the spare cash for A Company who had run short. I understand that he displayed his temper when he found out that this young Officer had parted with this extra cash. However what little cash there was left he took and the other chaps were unsuccessful in obtaining any extra pay. I should imagine that when that Officer paid out next and someone wanted extra pay it would be like drawing blood out of a stone.

That night in the Public House we did not drink anything so common as vin blonk – we were wealthy so each speculated on a bottle of champagne.

· · ·

The next morning we were out by six-thirty – all were to be on parade at 7.30 for rifle inspection. There was one fellow cleaning his buttons while another would be polishing his boots – how strange these things seemed to be after being subject to hunger and starvation and being a human target for the Boche – it appeared as though we were in another world. It does not take a deal of imagination to realize the state we had been in when I say that for three whole weeks we had never had our clothes off – when they got wet and covered with mud they had to dry on us – wandering about day and night covered in mud from head to foot looking more like savages. Now here we were with our battalion and after twenty four hours had got to be on parade spic and span for rifle inspection. We were placed in the ninth platoon and the Officer commenced to examine the rifles.

Chester was the first for inspection – he had a new rifle, and its barrel shone like silver. With six long service stripes on his sleeve denoting twelve years service, he looked smart. He of course satisfied the Officer's requirements. Bill's rifle and mine had had a rough time and looked in a dilapidated condition when compared with Chester's. We were 'called over the coals' but our explanation why the rifles were in such a condition was deemed to be satisfactory.

After the inspection was over we had half an hour at physical jerks. "Who the Hell gave instructions for physical jerks in France before breakfast? He ought to be shot," I thought to myself. Another hour in bed would have done us more good.

Immediately before we were dismissed for breakfast Captain Kay put in an appearance with a paper in his hands. They were orders for the day.

He addressed us: "Men, all the battalion are parading to-day for a very important event at 9.30. All of you will be on your best behaviour and look your best. One more thing I have great pleasure in saying that Private Charles Jack Weetley, perhaps better known as Chester is promoted to Corporal as from to-day. He will take up his duties at once and remain in the ninth platoon Company dismiss."

"Good God – Chester a Corporal!" I exclaimed as I looked at Bill in amazement, he at the same time looking at me simply staggered. Chester stood there grinning.

"What's up? Ain't the first time I've been a Corporal – this makes the fifth time – I shall have to try and hold it this time if I can."

"Five times Corporal?" I queried.

"Yes. Five times. But there's generally been something happened so I got reduced again. The longest I ever reigned was nearly six months."

At nine-thirty the whole battalion was on parade – Chester with two new stripes on his arm stood at the head of the ninth platoon with the Sergeant, the Officer in front. In front of each of the Four Companies sat a Captain on horseback. Apparently all were waiting for the Commanding Officer and Adjutant to put in an appearance. At the head of the Battalion stood the Regimental Sergeant Major waiting the approach of the Commanding Officer to call the whole battalion to attention. They both appeared on horseback and when they were about a distance of twenty yards away the Regimental Sergeant Major in a voice like thunder, called the whole battalion to attention and then turned and smartly saluted the Commanding Officer, saying, "All correct, Sir." The Commanding Officer saluted back and came a little nearer to us. Captain Kay's horse reared up but was soon under control again.

The Commanding Officer fronted us saying, "Battalion, to-day is a proud day for us all. I have a certain number of awards. The medals have been won in the last rearguard action in which we have been fighting. Many I am sorry to say are no longer with us, the few who are, well know the horror and terrible privations which we all had to suffer. I say this believing we have seen the worst – each day we are getting stronger and stronger and I don't think the day is far distant when the Boche will be crushed. As I gaze this morning on the battalion I see many strange faces all just out from home to reinforce us. I know for the honour of the battalion you will all do your duty so that the sacrifices that have been made won't be in vain. Also as a reward in addition to the medals the whole battalion is being taken out of action and is going somewhere in the South of France for a few days' complete rest. I will now award the medals."

"Myself I have won the D.S.O., Major Thorburn the M.C., Captain Kay the D.S.O., Captain Brown the M.C." And so the awards were made – in fact every Officer received a medal. All the Sergeant Majors and Sergeants, a few Corporals and Lance Corporals and two privates each received a medal – I believe the privates were Officer's servants. We were then dismissed and Chester got very excited.

"Well, Blimey. Talk about medals coming up with rations. The old sod (the Sergeant Major) never went in the line at all and he's got a medal," he said. He remarked that Bill and I could not expect one – we had not seen enough fighting. To see medals being distributed in a wholesale manner such as they were doing rather riled us.

"Ah, well blast the medals! Hope they do somebody some good," I said.

We were now done for the day and nothing to do but rest or gamble.

The letters from home came up and I at once wondered if there were any for us – I was highly delighted to see that there were four for me and two for Bill. In a flash I knew who mine were from – they were from my mother – I would have known her writing anywhere. I read her letters through and by the tone of them I could see that she was very distracted at not having heard from me. Each letter conveyed the wish that I would write soon and was well. My poor mother – I wondered what she would have done if she could have but only knew the suffering I had been through. I felt relieved when I remembered the letter I had written her would possibly by this time be in her hands. The postman informed me that there was a parcel for me at the tent if I would go and fetch it. He said they had it ten days ago. When I obtained the parcel I was rather disappointed for it was in a dreadful condition – crushed and broken – just as if it had been all over France. It contained some home made cake and pastry but they were all broken into crumbs. There was however a sound tin of pineapples, box of cigarettes and a tin of insect powder and bug killer.

"What's that for?" asked Chester, referring to the last named article. I told him.

"Good lor' it's not a bit of good to the devils out here. It simply feeds them up. I know a bloke who put some in a match box and kept them in it a week and they fed on is till they busted."

"Don't matter. The cigarettes are just what we want and the pineapple will go down well at tea time."

All over the camp gambling was going on – Crown and Anchor, spinning jennys, unders and overs, housie-housie, nap, brag, solo, pontoon and even two chaps (they were London Bookmakers in civil life) were betting on two blue chats crawling between two match sticks!

We three were playing Crown and Anchor and the chap who was running it got broke and offered to sell the outfit for ten francs. Bill and Chester wanted to buy it so we could run it between us. The deal was done and we each put twenty francs in the bank to run it on. Chester said he would run it while Bill and I stand by in case there was a row and to keep our eyes open. Chester soon started playing with fire. It was a serious thing for an N.C.O. to be in charge of a gambling joint. It would soon mean losing his stripes, so we were compelled to keep a sharp look out.

"No limit on this board my lad. Roll up, roll up. Plonk it down thick and heavy. Come up here in your rags and go away in your Motor Cars. The more you put down the more you pick up. I'm little Johnnie Fairaway all the way from Holloway, never known to run away. Any more for any more before I lift the old lid up," he kept shouting.

We soon had a record crowd round us. We could trust old Chester. He was an old hand and this was not the first Crown and Anchor Board which he had run.

Bill could not stand the job assigned him. Standing on one side while others were gambling was more than he could put up with so he decided to go to another joint and have a gamble with them. This continued throughout the day until dark with the exception of meal times, when we ceased.

When it was too dark to see we packed up and went into the nearby village to one of the estaminets where the Crown and Anchor

Board was brought out again and we spent the rest of the night gambling and drinking.

CHAPTER XII

AT REST IN THE SOUTH OF FRANCE

EARLY next morning all were on the march – we walked about 14 kilometers until we arrived at a very pretty village where all were loaded into motor lorries. Mile after mile they took us. We were journeying South, miles away from the sound of all the guns and fighting.

We passed through the main street of a little town – shops were on both sides and people walking up and down the pavements doing their shopping. How queer all this peace and apparent contentment seemed. It did not look possible, as my mind flashed back to the things we had passed through – it made me wonder if it was War or whether it was all a dream. We continued on our journey and it was quite dark when we reached our destination.

We were billeted in a cosy barn where we stayed the rest of the night and played solo by candle light until 'lights out.' The next day we did not have to parade until nine o'clock – just in walking order for inspection then we were dismissed until the afternoon, when we played football. What a grand and glorious feeling it was to walk about free from worry and suspense – no rifles or equipment to carry about – not even a gas mask. We were right out of danger here – it was springtime and the weather was ideal. The grass in the meadows was plentiful and full of beautiful flowers. Never before had I seen such large dog-daisies and cowslips. All the hedges were covered with white May – birds were singing everywhere. In a little tree in the distance a pair of magpies had built a nest. A small stream ran through these meadows – its waters deep and pure containing a fair quantity of trout – they were rising every minute to reach the may-fly which was there in abundance. How I longed for my split cane fly rod – a trout rose with a mighty splash, it would weigh well over a pound. I thought what I should do if only I had my rod and fly case – how mad they are on the feed. My thoughts went back to a certain red letter day I had on Blagdon lake when I got amongst the four pounders. I wondered if those days would ever return – they seemed a long way off.

Bill and Chester have other thoughts – by fair means or foul they intended having a few of those trout.

"If we could only get hold of a few Mills bombs," said Bill as he had some scheme in his mind.

Myself being an enthusiastic angler I stood aghast. The very idea of blowing a trout up would be my last thought. No. Whatever happened I decided I would not be a party to this. I would sooner blow a few 'Jerries' up than those trout. We wended our way back to the barn where I left Bill and Chester as they made for the horse lines to try and 'square' the Corporal in charge to let them have a few bombs. Chester being a Corporal I had not the slightest doubt that he would be able to arrange matters. About twenty minutes later they came back for me and I was informed that they could not find the Corporal so they could get no bombs. I was glad. They did however, borrow a large net which was issued to be used to camouflage our guns when not in use. The net had never been put to the use it was intended for but the soldier they borrowed it from had used it for more than one purpose – he and his pal used to ensnare partridges at night when they were on the Somme. It was surprising the number of these birds there were about in that district in the autumn of 1917 –since then the net had been used as a hammock, and now it was to be utilised for fish poaching. Between one way and another these nets did more good than a benevolent Government could have done. Now that the foul idea of blowing the fish out of the water had fallen through I was quite willing to go with them and try to net a few. The net was large but light with very small mesh – just the thing for the job. We weighted the bottom of the net with stones to make it sink quickly and then we put it in the water and commenced to drag it up the stream. I stood about fifty yards farther up with a large pole making the water muddy. The bottom of the stream consisted chiefly of gravel and was beautifully clean – just right for dragging the net up. As Bill and Chester approached I could see that they had something in the net, judging by the expression on their faces. When they reached me Chester jumped across the brook to Bill which was narrow at this point. He was still holding the net and dragged it in line with the bank. The net was full of fish and we pulled our haul on to the bank. Although we lost a large number in the operation we succeeded in capturing about twenty. They were all good large fish and in splendid condition seeing that it was so early in the season. They were Rainbow Trout and mostly round about three pounds in weight. I had never seen such a grand sight in all my life – twenty specimen Rainbows all kicking on the bank.

In the midst of all the excitement who should come on the scene but the French Farmer on whose land I suppose we were on. There was as I expected, a row. He commenced to throw his arms about and shout in a typical French manner. He was shouting and raving like a madman, dancing round the fish. After he had said all he wanted he immediately went off into the village.

"That's done it, I expect he's going up to Headquarters to report us," I said.

"That's about it," Bill answered, "let's pack up quick and clear off."

The fish were put in the net and in about ten minutes we were down the transport lines again. It was quite easy for Corporal Weetley to 'square' the Corporal in charge of our cookhouse to fry the fish. He said he would clean them and fry them in one of the large pans if we would allow him to have one or two. They were to be ready at supper time.

The afternoon passed quietly away and nothing untoward happened and I naturally expected that we should hear nothing further about the fishing incident.

That evening three men in the C Company, ninth platoon had a grand supper of fish; their pink flesh delicately flavoured was done to a turn. That Corporal certainly did know how to cook fish. If all was well we decided that we should have some more the following day.

At nine-thirty next morning we were standing on parade and as the Captain approached I wondered if anything was the matter. I had the feeling that everything was not as it might be – I thought perhaps it was my guilty conscience but within one minute my worst fears were realized.

"Corporal Weetley, Private Smith and Private Worthy you will go down Company Headquarters at once. Fall out," were the words fired at us. "Sergeant Norman march the men down and wait down there while I arrive," continued the Captain.

We were marched down to the village street with the Sergeant in charge. He halted outside a small cottage which I supposed acted at the Headquarters of Captain Kay

"What's up?" said Chester to the Sergeant. He not being a bad sort was willing to talk.

"Can't quite make heads or tails out of it. An old 'froggy' made a complaint yesterday when I was in here (pointing to the Headquarters) said he caught three chaps netting his private trout stream and what's more the first night the battalion was down here he lost half his fowls – all his pigeons and a few tame rabbits," came the reply.

The Captain arrived and we were marched inside. Our Captain, thank God, is a gentleman. He gave us a good talking to. He believed us when we said that we knew nothing about the poultry disappearing but pointed out that French interests, especially when they are in residence must be protected.

"I am sorry, Corporal Weetley, you will be reduced to the ranks and you all will have twenty-one days pay stopped." In a few minutes we were outside and we wondered who had given us away. Chester did not worry in the slightest – in fact I think he was rather glad to be relieved of the responsibilities of Corporal.

Many times during the following days we thought of those trout but we dare not go there again.

Four days of complete rest and contentment we spent in this delightful little village but on the morning of the fifth after a march of many kilometers we were loaded up in cattle trucks and wagons on rail en-route once more for the front.

CHAPTER XIII

DOWN YPRES WAY

IT was pitch dark and for several hours we had been struggling to get up to the line. Rain was falling heavily –it always seemed to be raining in this part of the world. Everywhere was a sea of stinking, slippery mud and water. Shell holes, miles and miles of them, were all full of the black slimy stuff. The stench was awful, not only from the wicked black mud and slime, but from the dead – men and horses by tens of thousands had been buried here during the last four years. As we walked along the mud splashed up our legs, and as we slipped and slithered about it would fly in all directions, landing on someone's clothes – sucking almost like glue – stinking almost enough to kill us.

Here had been buried English, Indians, French, Germans, horses and equipment not more than eighteen inches below the surface. With the years of machine gun and big gun fire and torrential rains one can easily imagine that these men and horses buried here were in many cases showing out of their graves – here and there could be seen an arm – a leg – or a piece of horse which had been blown to bits. All over this sector such things were common sights – so what with mud, rain, dead men and horses, shell and machine gun fire from the enemy, and the awful smell, this part of the line was indeed a Hell upon Earth.

We kept plodding along and passed over some slippery duck boards. Someone tripped up over a stretch of barbed wire – a mighty splash was heard – then some poor devil was rescued dripping wet from head to foot

The rain was pelting down mercilessly, but still steady progress was made, and after a few more of our fellows had been dragged out of shell holes full of water we arrived at our destination.

The fellows whom we relieved were soon out of this Hell, and were back behind the lines.

The rain still kept tumbling down as though we had not had any for twelve months and the trenches we went into were over a foot deep, and with the help of the mud we were up to our knees in it. Bill stood swearing and muttering to himself.

Chester was crouching on the top – that was much too dangerous to my liking but he evidently preferred risking a bullet through his head to standing in water and mud. I sometimes wondered whether or not it was the wisest thing to do – even death could have been welcomed under such conditions. Soon a burst of machine gun fire made him jump back into the trench – he fell flat into the water making a splash so that some of us got 'eyesful.'

During this night we stood in the trenches shivering and 'quaking' until the early hours of the morning. Thank God by then it had left off raining. I was so cold that I felt as though I had no feet at all.

By daybreak we found that there was a quantity of buckets available and we at once commenced to empty the trench. God only knew how many tons of stinking water each one of us threw out – for three hours we all worked like slaves before we made any impression on it and eventually we were near emptying the trench when a further stench came to our nostrils. Where was this stink coming from? We very soon found out – the bottom of the trench was made up with bully beef tins which had never been opened. They had been there so long that many were bursting open – being rusted through. Didn't that rotten meat 'talk!' We shovelled a good deal of it up but the more we disturbed it the worse the stench.

Everything we touched was slimy – it clung to our hands and clothes. Bill's rifle was even jammed with it.

"Well if this ain't the bloody limit!" he said as he fired a shot over the top to clear the barrel.

Everywhere was a sea of mud, water and barbed wire – all that seemed to thrive were the rats – there were thousands of the slimy devils messing about. They must have carried all manner of diseases about with them – they were nearly all suffering from mange. Their only food were the dead and bits dropped by the troops. We threw a piece of bread out of the trench on the parapet – instantly a grey brute rushed out from somewhere and commenced to eat it ravenously. It sat on its hind legs. I slipped back the bolt of my rifle and took careful aim. I caught the brute right in the neck, killing it instantly. Towards dinner time (although there was no dinner for us) it became very hot and the heat made everything smell ten times worse. If we could have only got out of the trench it would not have been so bad but on this front it was far too dangerous.

Everyone had drunk their scanty allowance of water and my throat was like fire. I knew we had to wait at least until sometime in the night before we could hope to get a drink of anything.

"If this ain't enough to kill Hell, I don't know what it," said Bill.

Anybody got a 'blinder'?"

"Here's one," I said, "but how you can smoke being parched up like this, b-----d if I know."

"Well if somebody don't smoke to help keep this rotten stink down a bit we shall all have fever."

Well there was a bit of sense in that, but how slowly the hours of the afternoon and evening seemed to go! It seemed as though they never would pass by. However, thank goodness, darkness fell at last. Never had I prayed for the night to come so much as I did that day.

'Jerry' started to shell very heavy but I did not care what happened as long as we were able to get a drink.

A little later a dozen or more of us were sent back to help bring the rations up. What a blasted job it was to keep on our feet, but at last we reached our destination. We were soon loaded up – some with bread – others with pots of Jam – two carrying a large dixie of rice. Bill and I clicked out very badly this time –between us we had a large box of ammunition to carry back.

The Boche was still shelling and sending over plenty of machine gun bullets which made getting back all the more difficult.

All went well until we were going over some slippery duck boards when a shell dropped very close. All dropped flat on the ground with the exception of myself – I slipped in six feet of water and slime. Bill soon dragged me out. I heard someone say, "It's only one of the ammunition chaps who's gone in. No grub went in with him, thank God."

The remainder of the party carried on, leaving Bill and me to get back as best we could. I can hardly describe how I did feel. My trousers were full of slime, and mud was clinging to my kit. As I moved, water ran out of my boots. It was no use standing where we were – we had got to get back to our trench. Bill thought the best thing to do would be to 'lose' the box of ammunition in the shell hole he had just dragged me out of –it would save a lot of trouble. He picked up the box and dropped it in six feet of water. That was good-bye to that for ever.

In about a quarter of an hour we were standing in the trench again with Bill eating cold rice and plum and apple jam.

I could still feel the slime slowly dripping down my legs. Towards midnight it became very cold and I had to keep running up and down the trench to gain warmth.

About an hour before daybreak the following morning the German guns went mad again. The Boche 'swiped' our trenches with his shells, many of them being of the deadly gas variety.

Gas was everywhere – the air was thick with it. It always hung about more in these low wet quarters. Everyone was now in their masks, straining their eyes for possible danger. This was a likely time for an attack. A shell fell fifty yards lower down right in our trench. According to the cries for help many must have been killed and wounded. The gas got worse. Everyone who a few hours previously had prayed for the night were clamouring for the light of day. Nothing was worse than gas at night.

Our Lewis Gun a little higher up commenced to fire. They had evidently seen something, but in time word came down the line that it was a false alarm. So the suspense went on and on.

The glasses in my mask went misty. I could hardly see anything. What was wrong? God, what should I do? The oxygen in the decanter was giving out. It must have been the fall in the water which did the damage. My breathing was irregular. I clutched hold of Bill's arm and released my mouthpiece slightly and shouted out to him my trouble. Bill's mask was quite O.K. He took his mouthpiece right out and spoke to me quite naturally.

We quickly made our way down the trench, hoping to find somebody dead. It was again a case of the dead to help the living. I must have the mask off a dead man.

We ran as fast as the mud and slush would allow us to. In a few minutes we were at the spot where the shell had dropped in. Several wounded men were being carried away. My heart sank – it did not look as though anyone had been killed. I now knew that if I did not soon have a fresh gas mask I would be done for. Bill was several yards in front and like a flash he jumped on top of the trench where several dead men were lying with their gas masks on. They had been cleared out of the trench in order to give the wounded a chance to be bandaged up.

Bill worked hard to get the mask off one of the dead fellows. Something was holding it on. It was the mouth piece in the corpse's mouth. He had died with his teeth clenched and holding it with a vice like grip.

Desperate situations meant desperate deeds. Bill whipped his bayonet out and forced it between the dead man's two sets of teeth and levered them apart. The mask was then freed. I began to feel the strain – my breath was coming in small gasps –my lungs felt as though they would burst, but thanks to Bill in a few more seconds I was fitted with the fresh mask.

Feeling very 'shaky,' Bill helped me along to the part of the trench we had come from. I felt very queer. I had no doubt got some gas down me and in addition having fallen into the shell hole of water it tended to make matters worse.

I sat in the bottom of the trench on a petrol tin utterly worn out and fell asleep. I did not hear the rats as they scampered over me, nor the remainder of the Boche shelling. I slept till nearly eight o'clock that morning.

Thank God that night we got relieved.

CHAPTER XIV

THE RAID AT LONE TREE POST

ONCE again we have arrived at the front line and were put in 'posts' which were short trenches holding anything from 10 to 20 men and were about a hundred yards or a little more away from each other.

The German front line was about a thousand yards away and they were also in posts. On this front the day of heavy entrenchments had gone and in their place was what was known as open warfare. No barbed wire entanglements had as yet been erected and everywhere crops were in full growth – the wheat was about one foot high and potatoes and peas and the like were well through the ground. The whole of the ground for miles around had been cultivated immediately prior to 'Jerry's' Big Push. It was just before dawn when we relieved the Bedfordshire Regiment and from what they told us this front had a bad reputation. They told us that 'Jerry' used to trench mortar our lines like hell first thing each morning and last thing at night and what was worse the men out of several posts had mysteriously disappeared.

The Boche no doubt had fetched one lot each night for the last three nights but strange enough no one heard any movements and it did not seem possible that a band of about 10 to 15 men could be taken prisoners without any of our other posts hearing anything. Many of the men were very nervy, so unnerving was the whole business. Our battalion went in that morning, each platoon having extra machine guns and all the men having Mills bombs and some rifle grenades. Orders were that no one was to go to sleep at night – every man was to keep watch all night and if 'Jerry' came, and whichever post he was going to tackle, they were to give him a 'warm welcome.'

He had been the last three nights, so we had not the slightest doubt but what he would come again this night in an attempt to capture another post.

All had strict orders to keep quiet and not show themselves too much in the daylight as it was desirable that the Germans should not know that fresh troops had occupied the posts.

At stand-to that morning sure enough over came the trench mortars shells of destruction. One dropped in number 4 Post and the whole of the troops were blown to pieces. If this was going to be kept up every morning and night I thought we should be lucky if we ever got out of our trench alive. About six o'clock matters had quietened down considerably.

Although orders had been given that no one was to show themselves, trust an Englishman to sit shivering in a trench all day if there was half a chance to get out and have a look round.

By nine o'clock at least a score or more of our men were seen messing about on the top. One party of our men had gone out into 'no man's land' to a farmhouse to have a look round there, while others had gone out to a potato patch to scratch up a few small new potatoes. One soldier came over to our post to see if a certain one of his pals was with us in order that he could borrow a few francs for gambling purposes. Many of those who had disobeyed orders made matters worse by continually shouting to one another. The Germans eventually saw them crawling about and a machine gun swept the surface of the land. Everyone then disappeared like magic, and not a soul was to be seen or a sound to be heard. The firing ceased, and as I peeped over the top of the trench all was quiet and no one in sight. So securely hidden were our chaps that one would have thought that there was not a sign of humanity for miles around, but in less than a quarter of an hour all were continuing their quest. If there were any new potatoes about we meant having some, so Bill, Chester and I were soon a hundred yards in front of the line. We crawled through a patch of wheat on our hands and knees, Chester leading the way. We were making our way towards a patch of potatoes when all of a sudden

Chester stopped. Directly in front of him lay three dead Germans. They appeared to have been killed in one burst of machine gun fire and by their appearance they had been dead for some little time – the wheat had grown round them. They were still clutching hold of their rifles and their flesh had gone black – almost as black as ink. I do not suppose they had been disturbed since the moment they were shot dead. I immediately had visions of more Automatic revolvers and other souvenirs but when we got a little closer to them the smell was enough to kill a human being. We brought our bayonets into action by poking their pockets but there did not appear to be anything of consequence. Chester suggested that we turn them over to get at the back pockets, but when we moved them the smell was worse than ever. We thought that if we could find something useful on them we could put up with the smell. Each of us fixed our bayonets and firmly gripping the buts of our rifles placed the bayonet under the side of one of the dead and heaved him over in this manner. During this operation his head fell off his body – the flesh had gone dry and brittle so long had they been laying there. This made me shudder – what a sight to see a man's head fall off his body – it almost made me sick. Never before in my life had I seen anything more gruesome. Bill and Chester must have had hearts of iron for all they did was laugh.

"This poor old sod has said his last, I know," said Chester. We had all this trouble for nothing as we found that his pocket was empty. The other two were put through the same process but with the same result – I then thought that others must have been before us.

We went on further and I was truly thankful, as I could not have stood the awful smell much longer. We reached the potato patch and here again we used our bayonets. First we have used them to handle the dead and now we were using them in search of food. What a contrast! We dug up root after root of these potatoes – it was really a shame as we could not find any potatoes much larger than a shilling but in due course we had sufficient for our requirements and then made our way towards the post. Just then that machine gun started its work again and we were obliged to lie in the potato rows for a considerable time until all was quiet, then we reached our trench again all safe. We had to go back several hundred yards to a farm for dry wood for a fire. The house was empty so we had to knock a door down and take a portion of that back with us. We had our canteens with us and water was found in the bottom of a shell hole to enable us to boil the potatoes. The water, by the way, was the same as we used to clean them. A very small fire was made in the bottom of the trench, only practically splinters of wood being used which flared and made very little smoke if any at all. This was a long and tedious job but round about dinner time they were ready cooked. New potatoes were quite an added luxury to our menu of bully beef and biscuits. This sort of thing took place in practically every post which showed complete disregard for the Boche by the English when things were quiet. This was the very thing that Headquarters didn't wish to happen, as they did not want the cunning Germans to know fresh men were in the line. They desired them to come again at night so we could surprise him this time. These night raids worried Headquarters a good deal – they were done so cunningly, cleverly and quickly – furthermore they could not discover who was doing it all. For days the intelligence department hard watched this part of the front but could not locate what Division of Germans was in front of them. They knew where nearly every German Division was but these who were in front as yet they could not find out. They had missed a certain division of Bavarians from the Somme and they wondered if these might he them. This Division was one of Germany's very best, and thus made the British extra keen to know what had happened to them. They knew if we could surprise one of these night raids and get hold of one of the raiders either alive or dead they could soon find out all they wanted to know.

That dinner time Captain Kay came round, attended by his servant. Didn't he let off at all of us? He said that the next man he saw walking about on the top he would have a machine gun turned on him. Referring to some one he said, "Silly b-----, he hopes the Boche would fetch the blasted lot of us." It was unusual for him to speak like this – he always had such a cheerful word for all. Little did we dream that the Commanding Officer had been giving him a 'dressing down' for the way his Company was behaving in the line when they had received orders to keep quiet. Observers connected with the intelligence department had made complaints to the Commanding Officer and he had sent for Captain Kay to explain the reason for it all so the Captain had to go all round the Company and let all know that the Orders were very definite.

A Second Lieutenant who was supposed to be in charge a little way up the line got severely reprimanded. For the rest of the day a big improvement was seen and no one left their trench. It was beginning to get dark and we all were standing to. 'Jerry' commenced to send his 'minnies' over, and as they plunged into the ground making a crater of five to ten yards in diameter the earth fairly trembled. The British artillery had started to answer back – never before had I heard their fire so fierce. One of our Lewis Guns then fired a few bursts – a few Boche had been seen to move. In this uncertain light was one of their favourite times to attack. However, darkness came and nothing of much importance occurred. A short time passed by when the Boche began to send up Verey and other lights in the air and then his machine guns began to fire, no doubt to try and catch those of our troops who are on the prowl he knowing full well that more movement took place after dark than any other time of the day. Ammunition and rations had to be brought up and wiring had to be done, as well as other minor duties. Many a man was caught with one of the enemy's sudden night bursts. It would be about ten o'clock when rations came up – quite early for a change. Although we did not know it they were sent early for a purpose. The weather was fine but very dark and all was still – just right for a raid. Time slipped by and I thought that it would soon be midnight and something might soon happen – everyone was strung up and everyone spoke in whispers. Two Lewis Guns were ready for instant use – the gunners never leaving them a second. On the ledge, three parts the way up the trench, lay heaps of 'Mills.' Many a man would have liked a smoke but that was more than we dare do matters were now far too critical to take the slightest risk.

Something moved in front. What was it? We all heard a distinct noise – then came silence again. Two machine guns were pointed towards the direction which the sound came from – men stood motionless with bombs in their hands and others tightly gripped their rifles. Once again that noise. Something moved in the wheat – then came silence again. I could almost hear my heart beating as I gripped a bomb. Once more we heard this noise – this time it did not seem as if it could be more than ten yards away. Flesh and blood could not stand the strain any longer – the Lewis Guns roared out two whole pans of ammunition. The noise had hardly died away when a large black and white cat walked calmly into the trench, purring as happily as one could wish. This cat had been left behind some time ago when the French farmers were driven from their homes and since then its main food had been bully beef which our chaps had given it from time to time. How the damn thing put the wind up all of us, and no doubt the sudden firing must have upset the other posts. Ah, well! Thank God it was only a cat. We would sooner it be that than 'Jerries,' but probably Headquarters would sooner have had it been a raiding party from the Boche. After this, time went very slowly and it was just as if dawn would never break, but after what seemed an eternity we could see the welcome light just beginning to make an appearance. Although our eyelids were heavy for want of sleep we kept a sharp look out. Dawn broke but it was misty and soon the trench mortars got to work but as it happened on this particular morning their shells were going well over. The time would be about 6 o'clock and I felt relieved to think that we had got through this trying night unharmed. I wondered if all the other posts were safe. The Captain then put in an appearance to see what the firing had been about. He had hoped we had received a visit from 'Jerry.' Disappointment was written all over his face when we told him what our visitor was.

"Too much gadding about in the daylight – he's smelt a rat I expect – the cunning devils," he said, "but never mind we might get one to-night," he continued as he went away. Little did we realize what was in his mind. The day passed quietly away and we were only troubled once by a few 'whiz-bangs.' We had a few more potatoes in the middle of the morning then we had a little sleep, huddled up in the bottom of the trench in the afternoon. Night was soon on us again and that awful suspense then came into prominence. Nine long dreary hours were in front of us which would seem to last for ever. It was the terrible uncertainty that pulled us to bits. No wonder half the fellows we had just relieved suffered with broken nerves. They had held these posts for seven days and nights – poor devils. We were already feeling the strain when the second night had hardly started.

"Somebody coming!" I exclaimed.

"It's all right – only the Captain and two of his Officers," someone said.

"What's up – something I bet."

They came right in our post discussing a certain trench held by the Boche as 'Lone Tree Post.' It was known that he used this trench at night for more than one purpose –sometimes sending Verey lights up sometimes machine gunning and very often he used it for a listening post. It was such places as these where he often learnt some valuable information, such as movement of troops, which particular battalion was in the line at the present time, and more important, when they were going to be relieved. No wonder we were always shelled heavily when taking over. Always at night you could hear our troops shouting to one another in the ordinary course of events but the Germans could never be heard. Under those circumstances it was not surprising how the Boche got a good deal of information.

"Well, we'll leave things until after dinner," I heard the Captain say, "then you will find the men and I will meet you here at ten o'clock sharp. We must have plenty of time."

"Very good, sir," came the reply as they parted.

What we expected was going to happen. Instead of waiting in our trench for 'Jerry' to fetch us we were to go out and fetch one or more of them.

"Blast the intelligent people, if this is their game – but I expect it's got to be done," I remarked.

After all I think I would sooner go out after 'Jerry' than stay waiting and shivering in a blasted cold trench.

"How far do you think we shall have to go out before we find him," someone wanted to know.

"I don't know but I bet if the Captain's going out with us he'll keep out until he does find the devils."

"Have you ever been out on a raid, Chester?" I asked.

"Yes, by Christ I have. Ten of us an' a Officer –a good bloke as well, went out once down Arras way. We had got to get in his front line quick and grab one. We nearly got there but he was waiting for us and he killed eight of us and the Officer first swipe of his machine gun and me and a chap named 'Slim' Abbot had to lie in a shell hole until the next night before we dare go back."

"Good God! What happened when you got back?"

"Why another party went out the next night under a smoke screen and a big barrage. They lost practically all the men but somebody got back with a prisoner," he answered.

"That's very cheerful just when we are going out on one ourselves."

It was now exactly 9.40 p.m. when the Captain with two Officers came up. One Officer sent for all the men out of the two nearest posts to us and told them to come to this post with only their rifles, ammunition and a gas mask. We received similar orders and soon a party about forty strong gathered round. Some boxes of Mills bombs came up and each man took four bombs and then Captain Kay began to give us our Orders.

"Men we are going out to-night to get a prisoner somehow. Headquarters want one bad and I expect to get him at Lone Tree Post

– I know he hangs about there at night. If I don't find him at home there I don't know quite what we shall do. Anyrate we shall go on somewhere until we do get one, but for everyone's sake we must go out quiet. When we get several hundred yards out we shall break up into two parties. One will follow me and the other will follow Lieutenant Hamilton and we shall close round the post, when all shall make a dash in. As soon as you get hold of the prisoner, get back as quickly as possible, but get two if you can. If we happen to run into one of his night-raiding parties so much the better. Now, everyone ready. Good."

The night was one that was just suitable for a raid such as we were now to be engaged in. Dark with the exception of a fitful moon that seemed to cast a weird light whenever the storm clouds which passed quickly through the heavens were not covering it. We all knew we were going on a very dangerous mission and if discovered many of us would never return. The enemy were not to be underestimated for they were brave and crafty and we knew that if they had any suspicions they would trap us but we had full confidence in our Captain – he was a born leader of men and we also knew that the plans had been well laid. But with all this we made up our minds that if we were found out and there should be a fight we would not conic back without him no matter what happened.

For the first hundred yards or more the whole party quietly walked and then began to crawl. We passed that patch of wheat – the awful stench of human bodies which were still lying there rotting away was indescribable. The party halted – the Captain then went back to Lieutenant Hamilton to give him additional Orders. When he returned I noticed that he had his revolver drawn. We were soon on the move again, and commenced crawling through a field of peas. The rustle of the leaves seemed to make such a Hell of a noise. I was sure 'Jerry' would hear us. One of his machine guns commenced to fire and I could hear the bullets passing harmlessly over our heads. We were well over half way when we had another rest – crawling is hard work. We picked a few peas what few brief minutes we lay there.

Even the crunching of the peas between our teeth seemed to make a lot of noise. All our clothes were wet on account of the heavy dew.

On and on we crawled without a sound from any of the forty men until one coughed but was instantly smothered. Again we stopped and everything was still quite calm. At this point I should imagine we were about three parts of the way out. The Officer close to me looked at his illuminated wrist watch.

"Twenty to twelve," he whispered.

Nearly two hours had we been crawling – my back ached enough to break but still we had to go on.

"How much bloody farther?" asked Bill in a whisper. "Keep on like this we shall finish up in Berlin or somewhere else." The Boche machine gun started again – this time the reports were extremely loud and I gathered by this that we were not so very far away. We rested again. Our party was split up again – about half going with Lieut. Hamilton and the remainder staying with Captain Kay which included Bill, Chester and I.

As we lay flat on the ground we could discern a large trunk of a tree minus all its branches. That was our objective. Nearer and nearer we crept until the tree became plainly visible. Verey lights commenced to drop on our right.

Good God! What would have happened if one dropped amongst us? The enemy machine guns would have answered that question. Happily this did not occur.

In a moment we were on our feet and rushed towards this tree trunk – some from the front and others from behind. We rushed in on the Post but were doomed to disappointment and surprise – all our trouble had been in vain for not a single 'Jerry' was in the whole Post. There was, however, plenty of evidence to prove that it had been used at night but unfortunately he did not happen to be there on this particular occasion. On a ledge in the trench was a large stack of stick bombs and Verey lights and in a little dug-out at the end of the trench we found a magic lantern with a box of slides. What a strange thing to find!

It had by this time turned one o'clock and we were as far off our objective as ever. The Captain and the two Officers held a short conversation in the dug out. They decided to go on to another Post which was just in front of the recognized German Front Line. It was considered a certainty that this Post contained Germans and we were to go on a further hundred yards and then rush in but we had to do this much quicker as time was quickly passing by. We half crawled and half walked and in what seemed about ten minutes we were all bearing in on this Post, all of us with fixed bayonets.

To my utter amazement and relief we found two 'Jerries' in it half asleep. They never heard a sound until some of us were in their trench. They offered no resistance. They were taken prisoners. One was already on his way back to our lines with a dozen or more of our fellows behind him with fixed bayonets to push him along. The one who stayed behind refused to come with us and as we started to drag him along he commenced shouting at the top of his voice. That was sufficient to condemn him. A bayonet was slipped into his guts and we ran for our lives. The Germans in the front line perhaps would hear him shout and with that they would guess what was the matter. Never before had I run so fast. I knew I ran faster that morning than I did when I won a 100 yards sprint at just outside even time. The journey out to these Posts which took us hours to do was covered back under five minutes.

We all arrived back safely and did not receive any extra machine gun fire from 'Jerry' so I took it that he could not have heard us. What luck.

The Captain was very pleased with the way events had turned out and I could hear him say, "Well done men. Everyone has done splendid. I will see that a drop of rum comes up before daybreak, but keep your eyes open – the night is not over yet."

As promised the rum came up by the batman. I hated the black fiery stuff but it did warm you up and that was something to be thankful for. At 'Stand-to' that morning we had a hell of a time again. How he hammered our posts with his 'minnies,' B Company again clicking out badly, two posts being completely wiped out. No wonder the fellows who had vacated these trenches two days ago had no nerve left!

Five long weary days and five longer weary nights followed before we got relieved. How glad and thankful we were to get away from this Hell again.

We were relieved at about midnight. How quietly we cleared out of those trenches and how delighted we were to get back – what a Godsend it seemed to all of us, but the damned Boche knew we were leaving – he fairly peppered the trenches as we left and he also heavily shelled the roadway which we went down.

As the shells crashed down on the earth in the darkness, coming faster and faster, they seemed to be saying, "You have cheated me for a week but I'll have you yet before you get out." We hurried down the road as quickly as we could, the shells seeming as though they were following us and taking their dreadful toll. What rotten luck for those who had survived nearly a week of Hell to be killed when they had been relieved. We lost more men getting out that night than we did all the time we were in the front line. However an hour later we were at rest.

CHAPTER XV

AN OBSERVATION POST

WE were all about early the next morning when a runner from headquarters came in with the information that Privates Smith and Worthey had been transferred to the snipers section to fill vacancies which had been caused by two chaps being killed when we were in the front line the last time. We were instructed to pack up our kit at once as we were to go down the line for a few clays for a short course of schooling and to receive a special rifle fitted with telescopic sights. We had also to call at the Headquarters as soon as we had packed up to obtain our papers. What would happen next. Bill and I snipers. In any case I would sooner be in the snipers section than in a Lewis Gun team. You were not laden down with ammunition or a blasted heavy gun which fairly ate one's life away. We found out that we were to go to a village the other side of Aire and we were likely to be there for about a week. Poor old Chester did not like the idea of staying behind but there was no alternative for him. We made enquiries at the horse lines to see if there was any chance of a lift part of the way but there was nothing going in our direction so off the two of us started that morning on a long march.

As is usual it was nothing but moan, moan, moan, grumbling and swearing, mile after mile. We appeared to have covered a considerable distance but still we did not seem to get much nearer. Thank goodness towards dinner time we got a lift in a lorry which dropped us down in Aire just after one o'clock. This town seemed fairly large to me but there were not many civilians left. 'Jerry' shelled this place each night with his long distance guns. It was a Railway Centre so I presume that was the reason for the shelling.

It did not take us long to find the Y.M.C.A. which was in this place but the only thing they could offer us were a few biscuits and chocolates so we loaded ourselves up with these. Upon making enquiries we learnt that we had about fifteen kilometers to cover before we would reach our destination. We rested in the canteen until about four o'clock when we decided that we would go into the town and have a drink of beer. We walked right into the centre of this deserted place before we found an estaminet. As we were in funds made up from extra pay on the last pay day and the winnings from the Crown and Anchor Board we stayed until closing time. It was well past midnight when we reached the sniping school.

During the next four days most of our time was taken up in learning to fire through the new sights, passing other fire tests at figures up to six hundred yards range and having lessons in observation. The fifth day we were on our way back again, both with a satisfactory report from the school. Thanks to a ride in a lorry we arrived back quite early. The vehicle we rode in was taking shells up to a battery which was operating near where our battalion was at rest.

Immediately we arrived back the first thing that met our eyes was Chester sitting on the floor with a large crowd round him playing Crown and Anchor. Wasn't he pleased to see us back again? We found that he had been promoted again, not to the rank of Corporal this time, but in charge of the lavatories when the Company was out of the line. His duties consisted of digging holes and finding buckets but he was in lieu excused all parades. The job suited Chester down to the ground.

We soon gathered that the battalion was going in the lines again the following night. It was just our luck to get back in time for this. The following night came all too quickly and at ten o'clock we were on the march once again. We were going up that treacherous part of the line once more, just on the right of where we went in last time. The usual amount of shelling took place as we were taking over. To me it seemed the biggest mystery in the world how the Boche always knew every time these things were taking place. Fortunately we all got into the trenches safely and at once the Corporal of the sniping Section came round the post for Bill and I. He had six more fellows with him – two from each of the other three Companies and with this completing the battalion list of snipers.

The Corporal gave us the discouraging news that we were to go out into 'No man's land' to a farmhouse standing quite six hundred yards out. It was over half way between our line and those of the Boche and we were to stay there day and night to use it as an observation post. From a certain position in the roof a really good view of the Germans' posts could be had. We knew this would he tricky business and on no account in the daytime must we show ourselves as we knew full well that if we did it would soon be Good-bye when the Boche got his Artillery trained on the building. The house had never been used for this before and no doubt that was the reasons why it was still standing at this time.

All our Posts knew we were in front. We made our way out carefully and kept a sharp look out. It was quite easy to walk into one of 'Jerry's' parties at night prowling about looking for one thing or another. At last we reached the farmhouse – I really began to think we were never going to get there, so far out did it stand. I noticed we came through several good patches of potatoes and one patch of peas, many fit to gather. We had already decided that the night we went out we would take some of these green peas with us. It would soon be light. Thank goodness it would give us a chance to see where we were. So far all had been quiet.

At daybreak the Boche sent over the 'minnies,' of course going well over from where we were, dropping on some part of our front line post. They also sent over quite a lot of 'whiz-bangs' together with a few gas shells. To me it appeared as though the Enemy were very 'windy' on this sector. Who knows what might have happened in his front line since we were last here nearly a week ago? A lot of things could happen in a week, especially in the front line. Little did we dream that the battalion who relieved us a little higher up last week had been making night raids nearly every night. No need to wonder why the Boche was a little unsettled. It was now light enough to enable us to see. The house contained plenty of furniture but was in great disorder – a small piano stood in the corner of one room with all the keys knocked out – crockery lay broken all over the floor. On the table there was a German soldier's tin hat and a German newspaper. It therefore appeared that it was likely the Germans might visit this house even now – we had to be careful.

Outside a large wall ran round one side of the house, to make a yard for cattle, I suppose, in more peaceful times. A well was on the other side of the yard, with a bucket and chain for drawing water.

As it became lighter it was no longer safe to be outside – we might be seen. We went inside the house again and then climbed up into the attic and removed a slate from the roof. What a splendid view of the German front line we had. Not two hundred yards away was a large German trench. The Corporal gave us our orders – two of us at a time were to look through the hole in the roof while the other six rest and this was to go on day and night. The only difference being at night we had to stand just outside the open door and watch for possible danger instead of through the hole in the roof. Our position was so acute that not a minute could we afford to be unguarded. The two who were watching had to report any untoward incident immediately to the Corporal. Any movement they happened to see, however slight, had to be reported. Each night the Corporal and two of the men went back with his report and to get the next day's rations and thus the days passed away.

Although we knew there must be Germans in the trench just in front of us not a sign of one did we see until late one afternoon when we just caught a glimpse of the top of one of their tin hats. In a second it disappeared. We had a good pair of field glasses and although we could see over several rows of trenches that was the only German who has shown himself. They were as cunning as Indians. At about nine o'clock the Corporal and two others left us to send the report in and get the rations. They returned about eleven o'clock. The Corporal said that the Captain had given instructions to watch those trenches very carefully, especially first thing in the morning and last thing at night.

A German Sniper had been doing a lot of damage from a position somewhere out in 'no man's land' and his position up to now could not be located. The Captain thought we might spot him while he was taking up his position or leaving it.

It was well past midnight and on this particular night it was rather light and extremely quiet – too quiet for my liking. Bill and I, who were doing our two hours' guard, kept a sharp look out as we stood just inside the doorway when all of a sudden we heard a lot of trampling of feet. Somebody was coming, then in my mind I thought that it would be some of our fellows out 'on the prowl,' but then, they would hardly be so far out as this. Who on earth could it be? Bill slipped inside and awoke the other chaps from their sleep, and they hurried to the door, where we all stood still and quiet, wondering who our visitors would be. Soon figures began to appear from out of the darkness. We all felt highly strung. There was quite a large number of them. I gasped. They were Germans. What could we do? There would be about thirty or forty of them. We stood there with heavily beating hearts and as if we had been turned into stone. There was too many of them to engage them in fighting. If only we had a few bombs things might be better. On they came into the yard and I felt half relieved as I saw them make towards the well where they drew water and filled their water bottles. I wondered whether they would come into the house when they had filled their water bottles or whether they would go back to their own lines. I prayed for the latter. Many were carrying sacks which no doubt contained potatoes and green peas. They slowly began to move. They were coming into the house. What would happen? No. They're not. To my utter relief they made their way back to their posts.

All the time they were here I did not hear a single one of them speak although they were only twenty yards away. This goes to prove what a cunning old devil the Boche is.

It took us some time before we got over this terrible shock and narrow escape from death. "Well, this looks rosy," I thought to myself. "If we have visits like this it is only a matter of how long we will survive."

Just before daybreak, the Corporal, Bill and I went back into our lines and the Corporal reported to the Captain what had taken place. We were then told to get back before it got light and to send in another report of the day's happenings, no matter how small, early in the evening.

Several times during the day the Boche was sighted but each time he did not show himself sufficiently long enough to get a shot at him.

Late in the afternoon when things were quiet, strains of music played by a band could be heard coming from the direction somewhere at the rear of the German lines. It was plain to see that the German bands had to go up into the danger zone – a lot different to our battalion band.

Many a time our chaps had been up in the line for a long spell and when they had been relieved coming out tired, dirty and lousy, fed up with seeing sickly things, and perhaps had already walked ten miles from the front line, have been met by the band all spotlessly clean. They would strike up a lively march and expect us poor devils to keep that pace up and march to attention the last mile or two. Perhaps the Commanding Officer would be round the corner on horseback (the corner always a Hell of a way off) and he liked to see his men come out of the trenches in such good spirits. What blasted 'Red Tape!' Troops in good spirits? Yes, I don't think! Fancy expecting this from troops who have been sitting on the doorsteps of death for days on end. We had other things to think of, otherwise I believe we should have came out of the trenches dead or mad.

Our report went in after dark to the effect that there was slight movement of the Boche in the first post and smoke was sighted about one mile back on our right, otherwise nothing else was noticed.

That night the Corporal had a surprise. When he handed in his report to the Captain he found that there were a score of men waiting with bags of bombs and a Lewis Gun detailed to go back to the farmhouse with us. They were to wait for 'Jerry' if he was going to prowl about and were told to hide themselves in the house and outbuildings. If 'Jerry' came God help him! The orders were that if he came to the well for water as we expected him to, no one was to fire or throw a bomb until the Captain gave the signal. The signal was to be a bomb thrown by myself.

It was about twelve o'clock that night and sure enough the Germans came, but not the large party there was the previous night. Quite a small party came this time. They came into the yard and stood a minute as if they had heard something. Once I thought they were going to turn back but they did not and kept on to the well. I could now see them as plain as could be – there were eight of them. They were nearly there – then I heard the chain being lowered, and then... The Captain threw his bomb, which exploded, and almost simultaneously a score more arms sent forth a bomb each – I never heard such a noise in all my life. Twenty or so more bombs immediately followed. What happened to these eight Germans I do not know – there was too much smoke to see and furthermore the Captain ordered us back to the line right away. One can only assume that these fellows were blown to smithereens.

We of the Sniping section were also ordered back but it was only under heavy machine gun fire from the Boche. They would know what had happened and they could be relied upon to do their best to do to us as we had done to their troops. We did however manage to crawl back on our hands and knees – all the time with enemy machine gun bullets whizzing through the air over our heads. The Captain told the sniping section that we had to stay in the front lines this day as he did not think that farmhouse would be safe in the future. Personally I felt certain that it would be a death trap for any of our troops to be there after this. However that morning 'Jerry' soon had his own back. The enemy artillery was trained on the building and it was not many minutes before it was struck direct by one shell. It was then Good-bye Farmhouse. Nothing stood now except one wall – the rest of the building could best be described as one large heap of bricks. 'Jerry' would no doubt hope we were in the building.

The remainder of the day was quiet and Bill and I got a little sleep in the bottom of the trench.

That night the Corporal called for Bill and myself. The three of us were detailed to go out to the ruins of the farmhouse and build ourselves a bit of a hiding place. It still had to be used as an observation post. Its position was ideal. The Captain said that he did not think we would be troubled with the Boche Artillery provided we did not show ourselves. I had the feeling that being a sniper of the Company was not going to be exactly a picnic. The usual precautions were taken and each post was informed that we were going out.

We again had to wend our way over this ground to the farmhouse ruins – this time we all felt 'windy' as we knew perfectly well that if we were discovered we should never return. When we arrived at the ruins it would be about 11 o'clock and as soon as we got into the yard, or at any rate what little there was left of it, I could smell the dead. We were all suffering from nerves. What a feeling I had – I wished that by some magic wand that I could be taken away from it all. To stand amongst these ruins and pieces of dead Germans which began to smell through exposure and quite prepared for death at any moment was sufficient to send any human being mad.

Good God! Something moved. I plainly heard it – we approached carefully the place from which the noise came. Something scrambled from underneath my feet. I thought how foolish I was to get the wind up when I saw it was only rats who were there feeding on the dead Germans. All night long these rats could be heard running about. They were like many human beings. They were starving and would almost eat anything.

It was too dark to see to do anything so we decided to wait until morning until we built ourselves a shelter, so we all crouched against the wall, waiting and listening until dawn broke. As soon as we could see we found out that we could not do better than stay right under the wall – we were completely out of sight of anyone who was in front of us. "What a hell of a mess he made of the place but then what a mess we made of those eight 'Jerries'," I thought to myself. They could not be called bodies – here and there could be seen a leg, or a head. I remember seeing an arm with a cheap wrist watch still on it.

"Oh, well. It's all in a day's work I expect," said Bill. "You never know when it's your turn coming."

Darkness would soon be on us again and we had nothing to report. Although we could see the enemy Post we were unable to see half so well as we could from the roof of the house before it was demolished. We put our heads together and decided to go and tell the Captain that the old ruins were no use for a sniping post. That night we made our report out but it transpired that excuses were not necessary as we were being relieved at about one o'clock.

Several weeks later we were again up this Sector but we had gained several thousand yards of ground –the old farmhouse ruins were still there but this time behind our lines. We went over to the ruins and had a look at our place of memories and as I half expected the remains of those 'Jerries' still laid there rotting away in the hot sunshine. We looked down the well and there could see some German equipment floating about in the water. Poor Sods.

CHAPTER XVI

THE ALLIES ATTACK

SOON we would be in the middle of the summer. Bill and I by now were just as hardened soldiers or perhaps sinners as Chester. Many times had we been in the lines and an equal number of times did we come out safely but I am sorry to say all could not say this, as several times since the spring the whole battalion had to be completely made up afresh. Although we had only been out here several months we were some of the oldest members, so completely had the battalion suffered. We came out of the line one morning and we found while up there a black and tan whippet bitch with two black and white puppies about eight or nine weeks old in a disused tumbled down dug-out. She looked a good bred bitch. How she got there and to whom she belonged was a mystery to us and when we first found her she was as wild as a wolf, so long had she hid herself and her puppies. What she lived on was still a further mystery – she could not have been fed by soldiers – she was much too wild and it was almost impossible to get near her. We eventually captured her and she was as if mad, she barked and struggled to get away and continually tried to bite, but quite suddenly she tamed down. It was really marvellous how quickly she changed and by the morning when we were relieved I led her down the lines with me as though she had belonged to me all my life.

Miles we had to walk that hot summer morning but who should be waiting for us that particular day but the band and a little further on the Commanding Officer just because we did not want to see him on account of the dog. He was bound to turn up. There was nothing for it but to release her, but she had made friends and meant sticking to me. Two more of our fellows had a pup each. What was intended to do with them when we got out never entered one's head.

The band commenced playing the Colonel Bogey March and we were all marching to attention, the two fellows with the puppies carrying them in their arms. We had now passed the Commanding Officer and were walking ordinarily when he came up to the Captain and said, "Were those dogs born in the Regiment, Captain Kay?"

The Captain looked round instantly and said, "Yes sir."

The Commanding Officer looked quite pleased and even rode quite close to the fellows carrying the puppies saying something about "Good doggie, Good doggie."

Thanks to the Captain's tact we were able to keep the dog. We gave the pups away to some fellows belonging to a Gun Battery as we could not find enough food for the three of them.

No matter, whenever we were in the front line that dog never left me a yard. When we lay down at nights and put our coats over us for blankets she would always creep underneath and curl herself up before going to sleep with us. A finer guard no one could have wished for.

Things out in France were moving and no longer was the Boche in such supreme numbers as he was in the spring, the British and French Armies being reinforced by vast numbers of American troops.

By now the great allied attack had started on the entire front and 'Jerry' was now receiving a dose of his own medicine. Day and night he was being harassed by the great barrages of British gun fire – he was never allowed to rest a minute.

That evening orders came up – Everyone to be ready in fighting order at once. We had barely been out of the lines a day and were being sent straight back again. We were on the march again – these almost ceaseless marches which seemed to have no end. We had a long tramp in front of us. The heat, although it was evening, was oppressive.

About this time our Battalion was having a hard time – men

under their great handicaps were dropping out all along the road. The Captain who could have ridden his horse was walking – what an example! Men were walking along with their tunics undone and their tin hats on their rifle barrels and this was our condition as on we struggled.

A party of dirty Portuguese passed by – about thirty in all – riding in an old farm wagon which was slowly being drawn along by two poor worn out pieces of horse flesh. Their harness consisted of rope. The rope round their shoulders acted as collars and had cut right into their flesh. What terrible suffering these poor animals must have endured. It was about as much as they could do to draw that wagon load of dirty devils –looking as black as ink for the want of a shave and a wash, jeering and laughing at us as we struggled along. Rotten sods. No wonder our chaps used to 'mistake' the colours for those of the Boche. They never had been in the line since the spring.

Still we kept on our weary march. Darkness had fallen long ago when orders were given that we were to have half an hour's rest. Thank God! Every one was about done up. Little did we know that Headquarters were trying to get us up to the front before dawn so we could go over the top with a certain battalion of men belonging to a Midland Regiment.

Time flew by and we were on the move again-soon we would be in Nieppe Forest. This oak forest covered miles in area. The battalion could not go much farther – everyone was done up. Another halt was called. We learned that all idea of getting up to the line by dawn was abandoned. We would get up there sometime in the early hours of the morning.

That morning hundreds of guns commenced to fire from the forest. They put up one of the finest barrages of gun fire the world had ever known.

On the outskirts of the forest eighteen pounders stood practically wheel to wheel – 9 inch, 12 inch and 15 inch batteries all were there. They had been secretly accumulated here for days past.

The ground shook and the heavens seemed as though they must burst open. British Gunners and shells were grinding the town of Merville to dust. It was nearly daylight and still the shelling was as fierce as ever. I bet 'Jerry' had a hell of a time over there.

We moved off again and were getting nearer and nearer to those guns. The forest was so large that every hundred yards tracks led off to gun pits, battalion Headquarters and other places all marked by a large board with the description written on. We kept tramping on through the forest and soon we would be at the end. Trees here were fewer and many were laying flat on the ground – evidently smashed or broken by the enemy shell fire – others just the trunk remained looking more like ghosts than trees in this uncertain light. We were now about level with one battery. We could not hear ourselves speak and my head seemed as though it were opening and shutting – much more of this I should go mad. At this time a terrific battle was in full progress in the front line but the heavy artillery fire drowned all the noise of bombs and machine guns and consequently we knew nothing about it.

Our platoon at this time was in charge of an officer from the Royal Flying Corps – he had been brought down several times. It was an unusual thing to see an infantry Regiment being led by an Officer from the Flying Corp and this set dame rumour busy. No. He was not a coward, but he had lost all his nerves and could no longer fly, but nevertheless he was no more fit to be in charge of a platoon going into action than a donkey.

We would soon be clear of the wood and one of the chaps connected with the Gun Team dumped a quantity of machine gun ammunition into the ditch.

"Now you get that back straight away," said the Officer who was known to us as 'Flying Corps Harry.'

The Kid who was carrying the ammunition (I call him a kid because he would be only a boy of about 18 years of age) was about done up – he was completely worn out, tired and weary – he poor beggar looked as though he was about finished.

"Shan't fetch the bloody stuff out," he replied to the Officer. He ordered him again to pick up that ammunition, then he pleaded with him but it was all to no avail. The kid was done. He then turned to us asking one of us to carry it. We all declined. To our astonishment he picked it up himself and slung it over his shoulder and carried it as we continued our tramp.

Each platoon which consisted of about fifteen men was to advance towards Merville and each were about 150 yards apart.

We proceeded forward and all was quiet. The Captain came along and stated that he thought the Boche had gone back miles. Crops of wheat stood here five feet in height – it was perfectly ripe and its golden heads were drooping over for the want of cutting.

As we tramped on we came to a small stream and what a sight met our eyes. It would be about six yards wide and fairly deep. A plank had been thrown over at this point. Here several hundred dead bodies of a Midland Regiment lay. The bodies were heaped on top of one another. A 'Jerry' machine gun nest had occupied the other side this morning and they were holding the whole line up. These fellows had the task of taking this position, the job which we were to have done had we been able to get up in time.

Seeing all our troops heaped up as they were one can only form one idea that they were mown down by the German machine gun fire like hay falling before a mowing machine. We were grumbling over our long drag up to the front but there is not a shadow of doubt that this saved our lives. The lives of these gallant men must literally have been thrown away. They faced the wicked machine gun fire without standing an earthly chance. Eventually the nest of machine guns fell but it was only taken by sheer weight of numbers – 'Jerry' at this point could not kill our chaps fast enough to stem the tide. What a price to pay just for three guns and three dead 'Jerries,' and the position!

The stream was choked by dead bodies as they fell off the plank shot dead. The water of this stream which had hitherto been as clear as a crystal was now running red with blood – nothing more or less than a river of human blood. The sight was enough to make anyone sick, more especially as we had to walk on top of the dead bodies which were lying so thick that it was impossible to do otherwise – and so we proceeded.

CHAPTER XVII

A NIGHT OF HORRORS

WE went on about another mile when a burst of machine gun fire swept around us – 'Jerry' was just in front, somewhere in the corn. Two of our fellows dropped down wounded – they were shot somewhere in their bodies. Both only lived a few minutes.

We all lay flat on the ground and waited.

Other machine gun fire could be heard everywhere now – we had met the Boche much sooner that we had anticipated. Our Officer lay on the ground trembling the poor devil should never have been sent out. He was suffering from shell shock.

A trench was just on our left and we crawled into it for safety. It was a German trench and was quite eight feet deep. Whatever made Him dig so deep as this? Wheat stood all round and the trench was almost completely hidden.

There we waited and waited. What could we do? We could not see anything in front of us on account of the corn. It would simply be death to stand up now and look over the top. How far away was the next post to us? Of course no one knew and we then decided to stay where we were until dusk, then somebody was to go out and see what the position was.

The day passed by with machine gun fire from both sides. Neither could see the other's positions or trenches on account of the high corn. All the firing was guess work and if anything was hit it was merely luck and nothing else.

In front of us tracks had been made in the corn by the Boche in coming and going out of this post. That day seemed for ever but eventually darkness crept over us. Three of our fellows decided at once to go out to see how far the next post was away and whether we were to stay where we were or not.

They said they would be back in half an hour if all was well.

Time now seemed to slip along faster and it was pitch dark and our companions had not returned. What had happened to them I wondered.

The Boche was sending up an immense number of Verey lights this night. Many were going right over our trench, so near was he to us. Several patches of dried grass and straw was blazing.

Our dog which was with us began to whimper. Someone about in the corn I thought. We dared not fire in case it was our pals coming back, but time went on and no one appeared.

Our comrades had been away now quite two hours and we were all getting 'the wind up.' Two more of our chaps volunteered to go out and try their luck. Bill and Chester were also willing to go out on our left, which was the opposite direction to which the other three had gone. They were going to try and find out who was on our left.

Each of the two parties said they would be back in half an hour, whether they found anyone or not.

Just after they had left us a German machine gun almost directly in front of us commenced to fire and I wondered if they had heard anybody. The dog got very uneasy and started to growl again.

A Verey light dropped just over our trench – its weird light illuminating the whole countryside for fifty yards around.

Time quickly passed but no one came back. What could be the matter? The Officer said they had been gone over three quarters of an hour.

Still no one put in an appearance and just as suspense was at a breaking point, we heard a slight noise on our left and in another minute to everyone's great relief Bill and Chester came crawling out of the wheat.

They said they had been out quite five hundred yards but had not seen a sign of our own chaps but they had heard others in the wheat. Everywhere was swarming with the Boche.

"What's to he done? It looks as though we are in a hell of a mess," I said. No one seemed to be able to make any suggestions at the moment.

A small barn with thatched roof stood about twenty yards or more in front of us. Several Verey lights had been falling near this but one did eventually drop on the straw roof and in another minute the lot was well alight. To me it appeared to be a deliberate attempt to fire the place. The fire soon lit up a hundred yards of territory. This did not concern us much – we were wondering what had become of our comrades.

Something moved in front of us. We all distinctly heard it. The dog started to growl. Surely it was the other chaps coming back? We all listened intently but the minutes passed by and no one came in.

The barn was now burning fiercely and if we wanted to go back now it would he impossible to escape alive through the lighted area.

For our own safety we decided that we must fire our Lewis Gun now. The intermittent noises we had been hearing must be the Boche and who knew but what he was closing round us this very minute. Any minute he might dash in our trench or a few bombs might be lobbed over by some unseen hands – then it would be Good-bye.

Our pals never came back and after events proved they were just like others – they simply faded away and were never heard of again afterwards. They would no doubt be reported to their relatives as 'Missing.'

We mounted our machine gun on the top and began to blaze away – the bullets smashing their way through the corn. The rattle of our gun infused more confidence into us.

Our firing stopped the Verey lights for the time being at any rate. Then the worst happened – an egg bomb came whizzing over from somewhere. From where we did not know. Others followed but luckily for us not one fell in our trench. We sent over the top a few Mills, and then silence came again.

The fire from the barn was now dying out and we all decided that as soon as the fire had dimmed sufficiently we would get out of our trench and get back a bit. If we did not look out we might very easily have been surrounded.

The frightened condition of 'Flying Corps Harry' was appalling.

A Verey light dropped quite close to us and was followed by a few egg bombs. Our gun barked back in answer. This sort of thing went on for a considerable time. We soon considered it was time to dash back a few hundred yards.

Although the barn was still burning a little and making a certain amount of light we knew it would take hours before it died out completely.

We gathered our ammunition up and the Gunner slipped the gun on his shoulder and in another minute all of us were clearing quickly back through that tell tale light.

Just as we passed through the lighted area a man was found laying face downwards across the track which we were walking. He was a German Officer – no doubt dead. In those few seconds which we stood looking at him I noticed his spotless clothes a beautiful pair of shiny leggings or what I took to be such, and a wide white coloured sash across his back reaching from his shoulder to his waist belt. His left hand was stretched out and I observed he was wearing a light coloured glove. His other arm was doubled underneath his chest. We passed on wondering. Our thoughts were more on getting back than on searching that dead German.

A Verey light came sailing over and we all instantly dropped flat until it died down again.

Once more we got on the move and soon we were challenged. Thank God! Things are alright. They were our chaps.

I gathered that when we were in that post we were several hundred yards ahead of the others. We had gone into 'no man's land' close to the German post. It is one of the biggest wonders in the world he did not have the lot of us. Luck out here was a lot better than a lot of money and no luck.

In about an hour's time our artillery were once more pounding death into the German front line. Thousands of shells were coming from Nieppe Forest. They came so fast that it did not seem possible for a mouse to live, let alone human beings.

Bill thought we might go out carefully and have a look at that German Officer. While I hardly liked the idea of going so far out, as one did not know to a hundred yards or so where the Germans were, curiosity was so great that in a few minutes three of us and the dog were on our way. We arrived there alright and I know we were not mistaken about the place but we found that the body had disappeared. Not a sign of it could be seen anywhere. I knew none of our fellows had been out, then the truth dawned on me that the 'Jerry' Officer was not dead when we passed in the first instance. He must have been alive and shamming death. Who was he? What position did he hold? What was he doing there? No one will ever know. It was however, very strange, later when I told the Corporal in charge of the sniping section of the incident he thought he might have been a German Staff Officer but he could not say definitely. The German on his part must have thought himself lucky he did not have a bayonet slipped into his ribs. In a few minutes we were soon back with the other fellows.

That morning at 7.10 precisely the British attacked the Boche front lines. They offered very little resistance – our artillery having done the damage. Our shells must have played havoc, as it was very unusual for the Germans to fall back so easily as they did on this occasion.

The first Post our party took, had three Germans in it, with their hands up shouting something which we did not understand. We were about to take them prisoners when a fellow comes up from the rear and threw a Mills bomb amongst them.

"That's finished them off. Nobody minds," he said as he threw the bomb at them. That post was full of dead – it had received a direct hit from one of our eighteen pounders. As was usual we had to have a look round. In a small dug out at the end of the trench a German Officer lay dead – we also found a violin and bow in a case and a large quantity of music. Much of this looked like his own composition as they were written in ink and others only partly finished. Who knows? This man might have been a great musician. We all knew that Germany had the very best of her musicians on the War front on account of them being very quick to hear. They were put into listening posts in order to be able to detect any movement of the enemy quickly. But who was this German musician we found who prized his violin and music so much that he carried it with him even right up to the front lines? It suggests that he loved his violin so much that even in War he could not bear to be parted with it. Perhaps the violin which Bill was now holding was of great value – perhaps one of the old Italian Masters. What did that music say which was all in manuscript? Some finished – some only half finished. Was it some grand Opera or a splendid Sonata for violin? Anyhow he must have loved these things better than life itself. The world of music may now be a little poorer now he is gone, his violin silent, and his hand still.

We carried on and the Boche was retiring, leaving large quantities of ammunition, guns and stores behind.

The Germans were making desperate attempts to stay this terrific attack of the British. He had dug in this side of Merville and for a couple of days he held us up. Except at night they never ceased firing their machine guns. Sniping was going on from all sorts of positions – German snipers as well as British, firing from trees, stacks and many more positions.

The next morning the British commenced to send forth their terrific barrages on the German front lines. It was only a matter of time now – our line advances. Soon the Boche was in flight. How our Lewis Guns mowed them down as they ran along a cart road. As I looked through my telescopic sights with my range at three hundred yards each time I brought the arrow to the point as I pulled the trigger I knew there was one more German less. Bill was in his element and Chester never had such a chance in all his sixteen years in the colours. That evening we were relieved and fell back a little in reserve.

The next day our platoon had a rotton job to do. We had to go back a little to bury the dead. The weather was fearfully hot – for four whole days these fellows had laid exposed to the sun. Their flesh had all gone black and the odour was cruel. Many had been partly eaten by rats – thousands of them thrived on this quarter.

These men had been killed in full fighting Kit – even to a shovel affixed to their equipment on their backs. All the morning we dragged bodies out of the water to the nearest shell hole – they were buried in their kit just as they fell – as many as twenty being buried together in a single shell hole. Who knew anything about their identification discs? I wonder how many of these poor beggars are still 'Missing.' No white crosses of Flanders indicates their graves – they were simply buried without ceremony or fuss – worse than a dog.

Towards dinner time our thankless task was completed. In the afternoon by way of a change we had a game of pontoon in the bottom of a trench – others were getting up to all sorts of things – some were carrying their bayonet about with them hunting amongst the German dead. Some were firing German rifles to see how they compared with the British – another party were walking along the banks of the stream throwing bombs into the water to see how many fish they could kill. I am afraid their reward would be small as the stream had been done to death.

That night we had a lot of shelling to put up with.

Early next morning Merville fell. It was once a beautiful small town with some splendid shops and glorious old time Inns and buildings. It now lay practically smashed to pieces. Rows of houses were battered and broken up so completely that it was impossible to distinguish where the roads were or even where a row of dwellings had stood.

We entered the place in the middle of the morning, simply walking straight on over heaps of bricks and mortar.

The grave yard adjoining the Church had been simply churned up – gravestones torn out of the ground and smashed – even coffins had been disturbed and lay broken open, showing corpses which had been buried for many years. In one large vault which had suffered I noticed a coffin standing on its end in an upright position with the front half of the lid broken open and the corpse hanging out. Could destruction be worse anywhere? How we used to suffer under many of 'Jerry's' Barrages! - but they could not be compared with those the British were now putting up.

The Boche had left Merville and its vicinity heavily mined – mines were continually being fired for days after the enemy had vacated the town. One small bridge which had been mined went up just as a battery of our guns was being drawn over by horses – all were knocked out – pieces of horses, men, and gun carriages being blown in all directions.

The next day we were in the front lines again a few miles beyond Merville. In front of us were vast numbers of Germans deeply entrenched in several large cement 'Pill Boxes' full of machine guns which continually swept the countryside. The enemy also had many snipers out who, by the way met with a considerable amount of success. Although the two front lines were several hundred yards away communication between one post and another had to be done on hands and knees first thing in the morning and last thing at night. Tremendous Artillery duels used to take place. Our front line was shelled with his dreaded minnies or pigs as we used to call them.

An hour before daybreak a message came up for the sniping Corporal – he was wanted down at the Company Headquarters and I was to accompany him.

As we were about half way down the Boche opened his usual daily dose of minnies. We dodged here and there – sometimes walking and sometimes running.

We at last arrived at the Headquarters – which consisted merely of a small dug-out in the bottom of a trench. Here the Captain sat writing, smoking and with his cap off as if he was perfectly at home. The shelling was heavy and many were dropping quite close – I expected every minute that one would drop right in the trench blowing us to atoms.

We entered the dug-out and stood there, the Captain continuing his writing. Why did he not leave his work and attend to us so that we could get back under cover?

Crash!

That was another shell less than fifty yards away. Earth and other missiles were heard falling on top of the corrugated iron roof of the dug-out. The Captain did not take the slightest notice – he continued his writing and gave an extra puff at his cigarette.

He completed what he was doing and turned round to address us – he was as cool, calm and collected as though nothing was happening – I thought that he could not be human. I was more convinced than ever that nothing could frighten him.

"Corporal, there are snipers in front of C and D Company somewhere. One of them is doing a lot of damage. Yesterday he killed Lieut. Avery and four of his men. He also got two more in post 16. He has been enjoying this run of luck for several days and even before we took over this part of the line. Well, he's got to be stopped somehow. I want all our snipers to go out in 'no man's land' to watch all day and try to locate his position. Of course if you can get him so much the better, but as long as you can find his hiding place that is the main thing. We will soon settle him then."

We were all supplied with nets with a covering of artificial leaves to pull over us. Anyone with one of these over them at a distance even of twenty yards would be very hard to distinguish.

That morning before dawn nine snipers lay in various positions in front of our lines. All of us had telescopic sights on our rifles and each had a good pair of glasses. Bill and I were in a shell-hole about a hundred yards out.

All day long we kept a ceaseless look out for that sniper's hiding place. Looking through my glasses I could discern a structure in an oak tree several hundred yards off which might have been used by a sniper, but no one was there on this particular occasion. We could also see a position from which a party was firing a machine. But, as much as we had searched, night time came and we had discovered nothing whatever. Perhaps some of the other chaps had had better luck.

We met in Number 12 post as agreed but the other fellows were like us – they had not met with any success. All had failed, and to make matters worse the 'Jerry' sniper had in the meantime killed three more of our chaps, who were in a front line post and in addition had killed one of A Company snipers.

This sniper was putting terror into our chaps – never before had they to lie so low in the daytime. No gadding about on the top now going from post to post, everyone had to keep down. The slightest movement shown and a bullet would come whizzing over. What with 'Jerry's' machine guns, and Minnies and now this sniping business the front was simply a living Hell.

The next day we had orders to repeat the previous day's procedure. The worst was to happen – the sniping had continued and now the Corporal was dead. He had taken the place of another chap who had been killed the previous day and had gone out with one A Company sniper. No doubt the German Sniper or Snipers had their position weighed up.

We made another gloomy report. No fresh orders were given.

Early next morning the Captain came into our post with another Officer – a stranger to us – and enquired for Bill and I. He asked us to lead them to the post which was nearest to where the Corporal had been killed. The Officer, we soon found out had come up to deal with the Boche sniper whom we had failed to get. He soon set us to work.

We had to get twenty new sand bags, fill them, and build up a portion of the trench again. We packed them up extra neatly and he told us that we could rest until morning.

An hour after dawn that morning a figure peeped over those new sand bags. Instantly a bullet smashed its way straight through its head. Who ever fired that rifle is a crack shot. A few minutes later the figure peeped up again. Another shot rings out – this time missing the target which happened to be a dummy figure we had made to draw the Boche fire. This bullet entered the sand bag drilling a hole right through it. That hole was eventually to prove the sniper's death warrant.

A silver coloured round tube was inserted carefully though the hole and the officer peeped through. It showed a certain circle of ground about twenty yards in diameter. Who ever fired that shot was somewhere in that flat small portion of ground – it had narrowed itself down to that. Soon a keen look through our field glasses revealed a periscope which was protruding just above the ground at the end of a natural dyke.

The ground had not been disturbed and long grass stood all round. So that was where the Boche had been sending his messages of death from.

All that day the Officer stayed with us in that trench. No one could leave it and hope to be alive with the exception of under the cover of darkness.

That night an artillery Officer visited the post with the Captain. They were talking and obviously discussing the position of the German Sniper's Post.

They produced a map and in the dug-out they worked with the aid of a flash lamp a decision was reached.

Just before they left the Captain said to me, "You can watch that periscope at 9 o'clock to-morrow morning."

Later that night all of us were moved to another post.

At 9 o'clock next morning Bill and I were watching through our glasses on to the Boche Sniper's position. Precisely at 9 o'clock a Battery literally went mad. Shell after shell were crashing down – all within a hundred yards blotting out the whole countryside and churning the ground over and over. Not many of our chaps knew that two 'Jerries' had been blown to smithereens.

It cost thousands of pounds in shells alone to kill those two men, but the money was well spent. Sniping on that front had been stopped for ever.

CHAPTER XVIII

THE PILL BOX

THAT night Bill had a small parcel come up by the post. Chester and I shared in the good things – we each had a packet of Woodbines. "God Blimey, these blinders are a Godsend," said Chester, "the first we have had for over a week."

"Reminds yer of old times," remarked Bill, "I say how should yer like to see Tottenham Hotspur and Chelsea play Football again?"

"Shut your row. Talk about summat sensible," came the reply.

"Or what about a good show at the Coliseum?"

"Put a sock in it."

We soon found something to discuss. News came along that we were going over the top first thing in the morning.

"God streuth. They don't allow you time to breathe nowadays," said Bill.

"We'll be up here now a Hell of a time," I said, "I thought perhaps we should get relieved to night." No such luck came our way.

Just at daylight next morning all were waiting for the signal to go over. The artillery were going to give us a good barrage.

At the given time our entire front line jumped forward and were attacking the Germans – our artillery were putting up a raging fire on their posts – it did not look as though anything on earth could live while such fire was going on. There were plenty of shell holes and we rushed from one to another – nearer and nearer we got.

By this time our shells were falling right into the German lines. One of the Boche flanks gave out but the fire from the Pill Box was as fierce as ever – it was doing a tremendous amount of damage. We were just on the right. It looked as though the Germans were going to fight to the bitter end. We had to take cover and each of us lit a Woodbine – which finished the three packets. Our line went forward and in a few minutes we had the Pill Box surrounded.

In a matter of seconds a dozen or more of us jumped in from behind but were temporarily driven back by revolver fire from the loaders of the gun. It was a fight to the finish so we threw in a few Mills bombs which settled the argument. What brave men these few 'Jerries' were. Only six men manned that 'Pill Box.' Three men kept the gun going while the other three attempted to keep their fort intact by revolver fire.

Our chaps soon grabbed the revolvers – they were as good as money when down the line.

"What's that Bill. Chester is hit," I cried.

"Good God! Where is he?" shouted Bill as he pushed his way out of the Pill Box. I made a mad rush after him – Chester lay just outside the 'Pill Box' shot through the chest by a revolver bullet by one of the German Gunners. Bill knelt down by his side and produced his field bandages. I called out for a stretcher bearer. What was the good when across that stretch of open country over which we had just come, scores more of our chaps lay in similar need. They could not be everywhere at once.

Poor old Chester lay there groaning with his eyes shut. I was certain he was done. Where was a blasted stretcher so we could put him on and take him back quickly. I knew in the bottom of my heart I wished in vain. I held him up – Bill carefully undid his equipment and then his tunic. Yes, there was the wound. We laid the bandage on. No. It's no good – he was going.

"Chester, Chester, speak to us. Buck up old chap – you only

have a 'Blighty'," I said with a lump in my throat and tears in our eyes. He rallied – he opened his eyes – he was going to speak. We did not hear the German bullets whizzing round us – we did not even hear our own chaps shouting to us to get down. At this moment we had only one consideration and that was for our Pal.

Those eyes opened slowly and turned to Bill, then they turned to me as if he was trying to say something. The next moment they were closed – closed for ever.

We had to get on – the others were well ahead of us.

We covered less than half a mile and we had to dig in again.

Late that night in the moonlight two figures could be seen digging a grave. It was soon completed – a rough wooden cross marked the place of rest – the last resting place of our poor pal Chester – at least he was buried decently. That night as we sat sorrowfully in the bottom of our trench resting, we declared that we would shoot every bloody German on sight. Never had I felt so sick and fed up with everything as I did that night. It had been eighteen hours since last I ate anything – the food felt as though it would choke me.

Dawn broke and our guns started this hellish business again. It seemed as if nothing else existed in the world except Shells and Blood. If this was to be kept up I thought to myself there would soon be no one left.

We were put in the flying column and we were soon well aware of the fact. That is the mob to get killed in!

We attacked again like mad – the Boche was not allowed a moment's peace. We were creeping through corn – the bullets were clipping the ears off in thousands. Desperate, or even mad men were firing those German guns, the main German Army having retired leaving machine guns every hundred yards or so to hold up the British. The Gunners were promised to be relieved at night if they could hold out. Night never came for them – madly they were sweeping their gun fire at us – they certainly put up a wonderful display of courage, pluck and endurance but they must have known they were fighting a losing game. Slowly but surely we closed in on them. When they fired at our flanks the front crept forward and when he turned on our front the flank crept forward bringing death nearer and nearer, but in spite of all this we were paying a big price. Down went Sergeant Reeder with a bullet in his stomach. The stretcher bearers happened to be up now and they attended to his wound while under fire which was terrific from the gun which was just in front of us.

The German Gunner must have been aware that he had but only a few minutes to live and was doubtless determined to fight to the finish.

The stretcher bearers had to lie low while bandaging the Sergeant up and in a few minutes had him on the stretcher. They called for two volunteers. It was necessary for two men to get up and carry this wounded man. Everyone knew that to do this was asking for death – it was certain suicide to stand up in an attempt to undertake such a job as carrying away the stretcher shoulder high under such dreadful fire.

Two men volunteered. What madness, yet, what bravery! What courage! How many thousands of acts like this have gone unrewarded?

As they raised their burden shoulder high above the golden corn I expected every minute would be their last. The undreamed of happened. That German Gunner ceased firing. A wonderful act of Charity even in time of War. The German Gunner knew that any of our troops who attempted to stand up would meet certain death. Why did he stop firing? Why did he not kill these two fellows? I can only assume that he admired their courage or he had the greatest respect for the wounded.

Slowly the ambulance party made off and not until they were well out of sight did that German commence firing again. He had declared war once again knowing perfectly well that he had only a very short time to live – perhaps only a matter of seconds. Faster than ever he was swinging his gun round and round, bullets flashing through the air in all directions.

We had gathered round him when his gun 'gave out.' He flung it down and prepared to bolt. At that very moment fifty British bullets entered his body. He had done his duty nobly and well for his Country. He looked only a boy, not a day older than seventeen did he appear – he was like all the rest of the 'Jerries' on this part – half starved.

Our advance continued and later in the day a farmhouse and buildings containing four machine guns and something like twenty men were captured. They did not put up half the resistance that solitary youth did earlier on. They rushed out of the house all together and were all shot Dead – Bill and I faithfully upholding our vows which we had made the previous day.

Darkness spread, and found us digging in.

That night thank God we were relieved and went back a short distance into the reserve lines. The next day we learnt that we were going right out of action for a few days and then on to an entirely new front.

One hour before we were clue to leave Bill and I went to have a last look at Chester's grave.

CHAPTER XIX

LUCK DESERTS US

THE heat was intense. We were marching again – always the same old tale – plenty of dragging about. Many miles we had covered. Everyone was tired and weary. Who was not in this Hell of a Country! My shoulder straps were cutting into my flesh. Perspiration was pouring down me – lice were fairly eating my life away –my feet felt as though they were walking on red hot cinders.

Bill's condition was even worse. All had been marching since soon after dawn. We were making for a certain village which we were expected to reach before dinner time, then we should rest until the morrow when we should be loaded en-rail for an unknown destination. Then what was laying in store for us thank God nobody knew. I felt sad – things did not seem the same since we lost Chester. There was just that something missing.

We had been out now two days – my nerves were getting bad – as weary as I was I could not sleep at night – memories haunted me. I had that awful feeling that something was going to happen – I could not shake it off. Bill only laughed but he was not himself –even the dog seemed dejected.

The village which was 'just round the corner' ten miles back was reached. We flung ourselves down utterly worn out – we were billeted in a cowshed.

It must have been nearly dinner time – the smell of pork and beans reached my nostrils. After dinner we had to parade with only a towel for a bath and a clean shirt. Oh, the joy of the thoughts of a bath and a change!

We set off and instead of the washhouse being in the village as all expected we began the familiar tramp, tramp, tramp. Mile after mile again. Another of those 'just round the corner' stunts.

Everyone was exercising their greatest privilege of moaning and swearing, but the washhouse was reached at last – just a small structure where a barrel was placed in the air and you stood under it a few seconds and got a shower bath of dirty water.

I handed in my lice infested shirt and in exchange received a 'clean' one practically as bad. Bill got hold of a shirt which was in a dreadful condition and he had to change it.

"You have to mix the breed a bit but this one is too bad," he said.

Late that evening we arrived back – I suppose we were expected to be feeling well after our 'refreshing' bath. All were 'done up' and we bolted the cold tea which had been saved for us in the large dixie. Soon the majority had thrown themselves down on the floor of the cowshed, their aching bodies and sore feet resting until early morning when all would be on their way again. This country was certainly no place for a weakling.

Morning came all too quickly. A few more miles march and we found ourselves at a Rail head. The whole battalion was loaded up in trucks bound for somewhere on the Somme. For many hours that day the train slowly crawled along – stopping and starting, fair jolting our insides out. The train stopped against a farmhouse with a fine Orchard – several score of our chaps jumped off the train and made a lightning raid. Poor apple trees! They ruthlessly grabbed the fruit off. Soon all were in full flight with the farmer in pursuit. All scrambled into the trucks safely and mixed with the other fellows. One man to the French farmer is as good as another. The train started off again with a score of heads looking out of the doors making fun at the old Frenchman. As the train slowly went round the bend I could still see him standing there, raising his fists, and threatening what he would do if only he could lay his hands on the culprits.

That night we slept in some old disused trenches and early the next morning we were on our way up to the front line. This part of the line was new to us. "Will fate be kind to us?" I wondered. No building of any description remained standing on this part – all had been hammered flat years ago. No golden crops of corn or fields of potatoes and peas or trees to greet our eyes like we were accustomed to seeing on the front we had just left. Absolutely the reverse. Nothing but a vast wilderness of waste and broken ground – very little nature was left on top of it alive – only live men on top with plenty of dead ones underneath. Cemeteries were plentiful in this part of the country. We had seen two British and now there was one German. On and on we marched through this wilderness of death.

Observation balloons could be seen up in the sky and guns were heard doing their fiendish work.

Late that afternoon we lay in the reserve line ready to go up in the evening. The British on this front were attacking – our advance was continuing everywhere. Day and night our troops were dealing the enemy death blows. The bloodhounds of Britain were slowly but surely strangling him. His well organised lines were crumbling – the Germans were now beat and they knew it. It was just a matter of time – death and dysentery stared them in the face – their gaps were filled up by deserters and shirkers. They did not obey their Officers like they did a few months ago – they were tired of War. It was our turn now – we were the strongest – we had been reinforced by tens of thousands of splendid American troops – they were fresh and they were fit – not tired and weary of fighting and suffered hardships like we had. All these troops had been brought over under the very nose of the enemy submarines and not a single man had been lost.

The night was now pitch dark and we were on a sunken road. We were just going in the front line and the Germans were shelling it like Hell. We were on a different front but just the same old tale – he knew fresh troops were coming in – 'Whiz-bangs' were dropping everywhere and the weird noise of the gas shells as they struck the earth was sufficient to unnerve the strongest. Everyone had on gas masks and the din was terrific –shrapnel was flying everywhere – everyone was hampered in their movements by their gas masks. Many were being wounded and killed. Something touched my leg in the darkness. Oh, it was alright – it was just our faithful dog. Trust her not to lose us. Bill and I were sticking close together. My nerves which were once so good were now breaking – even flesh and blood has a limit in time of war. Oh, the dreadfulness of it all! Everywhere we went; always the same thing. The angels of death were with us that night. As the gas shells came whizzing over they seemed to bring a message – Was it from God or was it the whispering of the Devil? What ever was the matter with me. I had that queer feeling coming over me. Get on! Walk quicker! It does not matter about the shell holes if you cannot see, get on! Let's get in that trench for cover! Was I going mad? Was I imagining that I could hear and see things?

I was getting weaker – on the verge of collapse and a total wreck.

So we went on in the darkness, practically feeling our way. Gas was everywhere – I could just whiff the scented stuff through my mask. The dog was whimpering – the gas had got hold of the poor little devil. I picked it up in my arms. It was too late – one more life was gone.

I felt as if my mouthpiece was choking me – I should have liked to scream out. What would be the end of it all? I had that old 'don't care' feeling coming over me. Was life worth living to be continually going through this Hell. I still held the dog in my arms – the poor faithful creature – I was almost broken hearted. Bill took her from me and dumped her in a shell hole.

In a few more minutes we were in the front line – soon after this the British guns opened fire sending thousands and thousands of shells crashing into the enemy lines. The firing kept on – never abating one moment.

At dawn the whole line attacked once more – the crimson trail had begun.

All that day the Germans retreated leaving death and destruction behind. Not one prisoner did our battalion take – all were shot dead. What was the good of taking prisoners? They had to be fed! Who could bother to take them back to a prison Camp. Shoot the sods out of the way. That was the spirit!

Later in the day we were moved over to the left to relieve a certain battalion of colonials. There we found a long trench partly filled with dead Germans. Most of these had been killed by the bayonet. Little would 'Jerry' think when he was attacking in such superior numbers a few short months ago the tables would so completely be turned.

Soon we were right through the famous Hindenburg Line. What wonderful dug-outs! Here right down in the bowls of the earth tens of thousands of men could rest in these and be quite safe, but in spite of all these mighty lines of defence all were crumbling – the day of reckoning was fast approaching.

Darkness was once more upon us and another day of murder was past. How little value the life of a mere man was out here!

Rations came and we sat in the trenches eating – we ate all we could – we never knew what the morrow may bring forth – possibly no food would come up or possibly we would be dead. I ate and thought at the same time. How far away the old life seemed. I thought and thought, thought of my mother, my home, my pals, in fact anything so long as it was not this confounded blood and murder all the time. Tears came into my eyes. It was no good thinking about such things now.

It would soon be morning again and we were here to fight and kill, and to rest whenever possible.

A long and weary night passed and the British guns once more commenced firing but on this particular morning the Boche answered back. The earth tremoured and the heavens seemed as though they must burst open. The air was thick with smoke and flying shrapnel –

shells were dropping everywhere – the Boche was putting up a terrific machine gun fire – he knew we were about to attack. Shells were dropping just in front of us. Our luck could not hold out much longer! We crouched lower and lower – our run of luck had come to an end – a shell fell right in our post. Then came silence. Gas shells next began to fall. The British went over the top. They advanced – they went forward... but no one in our post knew anything about it.

. . .

    Hours must have passed – perhaps days – I do not know. How warm I felt! Where was I? Yes, there was Bill! He was not moving! All my comrades were still! What's the matter? They were all asleep of course! How nice I felt! Everything seemed miles away. I felt as though I was falling through space – I could still see Bill though.

    Why did he not say something? I was going again! How sleepy I felt! I was back at school again! Yes, there was Mr. Austin my headmaster! He was going to speak to me! I was playing for the first team! I must win! I must! I am still slipping! I could see my mother and father now, and little Billy! Yes, there's Oh, I am so sleepy !

. . .

    Where could I be – I could still see Bill! He still lay there – I must wake him up! Why do I not move? I feel in pain! He must be sleeping.

    I tried to call out but words would not come.

    Oh, what was the matter with us all? Why did not somebody come to me? What was it – night or day? I was going again! Where were you going? Oh, I don't know! I could see little Billy again and Chester – why didn't they come and talk to me? Oh, my skin was burning – I must have been on fire! Bill, Bill, do speak to me!

    Something seemed to appear in the clouds.

    What was it? I could sense its wings hovering over me! Was it a message from someone?... Good God it was a German! It was the one we killed on that road! He was speaking now – "Bill is dead – Bill is dead." He was going again! Speak Bill – do wake up! I was moving now – my hands were touching him! Thank God he was alive – he was warm! He moved then! Why did he not wake up! It was this blasted scented stuff of course. It was gas! Gas? What's that? Yes, I know! Put your mask on Bill! Bill still asleep? I will put it on you myself – now sleep in it – I will do the same! I was still sinking.

. . .

Stretcher bearers were picking the wounded up – the British had lost somewhat heavily this day. Red Cross Motors were running back loaded – they had been continually on the go since early morning.

"Why, here's a blasted trench full of our fellows," said a voice. "Well blow me – but I am afarin' we are all too late – they all look knocked out."

Someone else spoke. "Yes, he's dead, so's he – all this end look dead."

"What do you say? Two chaps your end got gas masks on and still alive? Good, let's get them back again."

Other helping hands were quickly on the spot. Just two more stretchers were on their way down the line to a waiting ambulance car. Two stood there each wanting one more case to complete their load. It only took them a matter of a few minutes to get a load. Both cars soon moved off – one taking the road to a field ambulance centre and the other going in another direction to a hospital.

. . .

I came round – I could just begin to discern things. I must have been in a large tent – wounded men lay everywhere. I began to see better but I did not see them take a number of dead men outside although one of them was next to me.

One more night's sleep and then the following morning another batch of dead were taken outside for burial. There had been slaughter again on this front.

I could not see Bill. That was funny. I saw him once I know – I put his gas mask on.

"Where's Bill?" I said to a fellow near me.

"Who's Bill?" came the answer. "If you mean that chap who lay next to you – he died yesterday morning." This fresh shock nearly killed me.

I was taken down to an American Hospital near La Havre where I lay hovering between life and death for weeks.

The great day came – La Havre to Southampton. Southampton to Glasgow – one of the greatest of all wishes. Blighty at last – one more step nearer home.

The War was finished – Germany was crushed.

I went back to that Eastern Command Depot for my discharge – no longer fit and well and marked A.1, but broken in nerve and my future life shortened. I am now a C.3 man.

I came up that familiar road from the station and there I met the old Sergeant Major. No longer did he hold any terrors for me. One more turn and I should be at the Headquarters. Some one just limped out – I seemed to know that figure.

It is! No it isn't! Yes, by heavens it's Bill! Dear old Bill! A few more steps and we should be together once more.

"Bill! Bill!" I shouted.

Bill stopped suddenly. He recognised my familiar voice.

In a moment we were together in each other's arms. "They told me you were dead, Bill," I said.

"Well, I thought that you were killed – they must have taken us to two different Hospitals."

We then related to each other the incidents which had taken place while we were parted, and our career ended at this Camp with a few happy days together.

I was now finished with the Army and War, and for the sake of humanity, I hope for ever.

THE END